Praise for
Shake It Off Leadership

Betsy's memories and thoughts are very engaging. The minute I started reading, I could relate to her feeling like a trailblazer and the need to take "chances jumping to life with both feet." The book offers exactly those directions seeking frank conversation about experiences that we don't talk about (childhood experiences of loss, family rejection, coming out in corporate America) and is well-timed. It read like a combination of self-reflection and management coaching with comments like "surrounding myself with talented honest people who help me make solid decisions," reminding us that business is indeed personal. It's well worth the read.

Maryland State Senator Mary L. Washington
@SenMaryW

Betsy writes a compelling story about how compromising your values is like compromising your soul and your whole being. She gives us a sneak preview into her life growing up with brothers and living in a household with a single parent, due to untimely death of her father. She forces you to look at yourself. She forces you to take a look in the mirror and come to terms with how you want to live your life and lead your company. Leaders lead leaders! You live how you lead and lead how you live. Lead on, Betsy!

Betty J. Holland Hines, Founder & CEO
W.E.W. Women Elevating Women

It is an honor to support Betsy Cerulo in her publication of her new book. She and I grew up in a time of incredible change in the acceptance of LGBTQ people. At the beginning of our lives' journey, we were forced to hide our sexual orientation for the sake of "fitting in." This added an extra level of stress to the already difficult time of starting a career. While advancing through the ranks of management, I think this hidden secret aided us in seeing things from a different perspective and gaining different insights into how corporate culture can affect the individual employee. Sharing these lessons is an important contribution to the management lexicon. Congratulations, Betsy, on your significant contribution.

Richard Larison, CEO
R&F International Hospital, Guangzhou, China

Shake It Off Leadership offers the deeply personal perspective of a leader who has learned to quickly recognize and disconnect from people who are toxic to productivity and happiness. These are two essentials to a healthy business or organizational culture and learning this lesson is a key to being a great leader.

Sam McClure, Executive Director
Chase Brexton Health Services LGBT Health Resource Center

As a CEO, a community organizer, an advocate, and a mentor, Betsy Cerulo continues to be a role model of strength and tenacity for so many. She shares her decades of leadership experience in *Shake It Off Leadership* in a series of inspiring, easily digestible anecdotes and lessons designed to focus your approach to success. The path to seizing your goals is not always straight nor pretty, but Betsy's words will help you find power in overcoming challenges and turn every obstacle into an opportunity to thrive.

Jonathan Lovitz
Diversity, Equity, and Inclusion Advocate
SVP of the National LGBT Chamber of Commerce

I am thrilled to have been asked to provide a testimonial for *Shake It Off Leadership*, especially since it came from someone who I admire who is a true leader in our community! Betsy embodies what I have recognized as leadership from my experiences as a U.S. Naval Academy graduate, a Marine Officer, a member of the business community, and throughout many years of nonprofit board leadership. Leaders transcend their industry or field of expertise in which they excel. You can identify leaders by the fact that they are asked to lead other entities even though they are not part of that industry. It has been my experience that leaders take us to places where we didn't know that we wanted to go to or, in some cases, believed it was possible to go. True leaders take an organization, a movement, or a unit to that next level as evidenced by CEOs, leaders like Dr. Martin Luther King, and many, many military leaders, officers, staff non-commissioned officers, and enlisted servicemen/women. Finally, as midshipmen at the U.S. Naval Academy, part of the prayer that we prayed contained the phrase "if I should miss the mark, give me courage to try again." Since we are all human and we occasionally do "miss the mark," true leaders bounce back from failures, hurdles, and setbacks by continuing the struggle to accomplish the mission that they have set out to achieve. Having known Betsy Cerulo since the mid-1990s, she has personified all of these traits and more, both in her business life and personally.

Franklin N. McNeil, Jr.
USNA Class of 1983; Former Marine Officer
Active Baltimore Nonprofit Member

Regardless of your career or the type of business you're in, there will, no doubt, come a time when you ask yourself, "What am I doing??? This will never work out. Why did I think I could do this?" Stumbling blocks, concrete walls, and BIG doubts can show up for everyone. In *Shake It Off Leadership*, business leader Betsy Cerulo shares how those doubts and sometimes crushing times showed up for her and how her resilience helped her to keep moving forward and keep her eyes and her heart on her dreams. The survival strategies shared to help navigate the ups and downs will help *anyone* get back on course and take it all the way. You'll be glad you have Betsy on your team.

Ann Quasman, Creator and Former Host
WomanTalk Live Radio in Baltimore, MD

I have known Betsy for most of the last decade and have always been impressed with her compassionate leadership and willingness to share with others. In her book *Shake It Off Leadership*, Betsy perfectly encapsulates something every one of us as a leader has experienced, failure. However, what really resonates is how she has moved beyond those failures to reach a new strata of success and how other leaders can do the same. Put this book on your must-read list and do it stat.

Justin Nelson
Co-Founder & President
National LGBT Chamber of Commerce® (NGLCC)

SHAKE IT OFF LEADERSHIP

•

SHAKE IT OFF LEADERSHIP

ACHIEVING SUCCESS THROUGH THE EYES OF OUR LABELS

BETSY CERULO

PYP

PUBLISH
YOUR
PURPOSE
PRESS

For permission requests, write to the publisher, addressed "Attention: Permissions Coordinator," at the address below.

Publish Your Purpose Press
141 Weston Street, #155
Hartford, CT, 06141

PUBLISH
YOUR
PURPOSE
PRESS

The opinions expressed by the Author are not necessarily those held by Publish Your Purpose Press.

Ordering Information: Quantity sales and special discounts are available on quantity purchases by corporations, associations, and others. For details, contact the publisher at orders@publishyourpurposepress.com.

Edited by: Heather B. Habelka
Cover design by: Matthew Gifford
Typeset by: Medlar Publishing Solutions Pvt Ltd., India

Printed in the United States of America.
ISBN: 978-1-946384-78-2 (paperback)
ISBN: 978-1-946384-82-9 (hardcover)
ISBN: 978-1-946384-83-6 (ebook)

Library of Congress Control Number: 2020905661

First edition, March 2021.

The information contained within this book is strictly for informational purposes. This publication contains the opinions and ideas of its author. It is intended to provide helpful and informative material on the subjects addressed in the publication. It is sold with the understanding that the author and publisher are not engaged in rendering medical, health, financial, legal, or any other kind of personal professional services in the book. The material may include information, products, or services by third parties. As such, the Author and Publisher do not assume responsibility or liability for any third-party material or opinions. The publisher is not responsible for websites (or their content) that are not owned by the publisher. Readers are advised to do their own due diligence when it comes to making decisions.

Publish Your Purpose Press works with authors, and aspiring authors, who have a story to tell and a brand to build. Do you have a book idea you would like us to consider publishing? Please visit PublishYourPurposePress.com for more information.

Disclaimer

The stories in this book have been written from the Author's recollections. They are not written to represent word-for-word transcripts of conversations or events. Rather, the Author has retold them in a way that evokes the feeling and meaning of what was said. In all instances the essence of the dialogue is accurate. However, names and identifying details have been changed to protect the privacy of the people involved.

I dedicate this book to my wife, Susan,
who believed in me when all my hope was gone.
You saved my life.

Table of Contents

III. NURTURING HEALTHY BUSINESS AND LIFE RELATIONSHIPS

IV. HEALTH

V. YOUR FINISH LINE

Foreword

*The future belongs to those who believe
in the beauty of their dreams.*

—Eleanor Roosevelt

Dear Gentle Reader,

Whatever you may believe has drawn you to read *Shake It Off Leadership*, know that at least part of the draw is that you are meant to be a part of our tribe—my tribe with this book's author, Betsy Cerulo.

Betsy and I first met in the winter of 1982, on a very cold January afternoon in northeast Washington, D.C., on the shabby pitch that served as The Catholic University of America's women's softball field. I was a sophomore and a recent transfer from the University of South Florida in Tampa. Betsy was a junior—fun, very amiable, and a student leader on my side of the campus. Over the months that followed our early practices and games that season, Betsy and I bonded and became friends because we had both confronted the same point of stupefying self-awareness: We had fallen in love with teammates on our small squad and, through this, we had discovered we were lesbians.

We were Catholic girls. In love with other Catholic girls. In conflict with Roman Catholic Church teachings and with our families' cultures, expectations, and dreams of who they (and we) believed we were meant to become.

Betsy's insights and guidance in the pages that follow are meant to guide you toward claiming and owning the labels that make you who you are. Betsy's wisdom in encouraging this approach to personal growth and leadership development has been hard-won, through decades of persevering, self-reflecting, learning, and forgiving herself when she came up short on her dreams.

However, in 1982 when we were first coming out, the labels I know we struggled with and struggled to claim were not the point of pride they have become for both of us over these past nearly four decades. To be a dyke meant we were outsiders. Less than. Sinners. I know I feared there was no hope for my future within the Church. And, worse, I feared there was no hope for a future within my tight Cuban/Spanish/Italian/Ciboney family. I carried such shame. Betsy was a lifeline the first summer after I came out because at least I had a friend with whom I could share this lonely, terrifying reality.

In the spring of my junior year, grace intervened for me in the form of Father Robert Friday, my junior year religion teacher. I was still struggling with accepting who I knew I was and desperate to reconcile being me with being a spiritual person within the Catholic Church. One afternoon after our class had concluded and he took time to hear my half-broken confession, Father Friday smiled at me and said in the most genuine and heartfelt way, "We are all made in the likeness of God, and God makes no mistakes." That kindness changed me and it changed my life.

I have often looked back at myself then and smiled many, many times. Doing that, smiling upon the young, scared 20-year-old, has proved repeatedly redeeming. It was then that I first began to claim that label—lesbian. In time, I became proud that I am a woman made in the likeness of God, who has loved women, and made my life with one woman and created a family for nearly

30 years. Of all the labels I wear, this is the one I believe I wear with the fullest pride because it was the first and hardest to claim and belongs to me alone.

▪ ▪ ▪

Wherever you may be in your personal or professional journey, Betsy's stories and this book serve as an invitation to pause and consider the treasure that is your lived experience and an opportunity to see it all from new angles. Claim the labels that you have worn in the past, but with a refreshed perspective. Examine the labels you have resisted and do so with compassion, courage, and curiosity. Discover new labels that inspire and energize your dreams. Whoever you may be: *Mother, daughter, father, son. Elder, believer, seeker, advocate. Survivor, striver, student, chief. Inventor, innovator, coach, steward.*

In my experience, each time I need to break out of a troubling old habit or belief system, break away from or understand a complicated relationship, or create a breakthrough in my personal, community, or professional work, I so often find gold when I mine the experiences of my past. I have sometimes found the labels I have given myself or assumed without real consideration. And often—too often—I discover that I have been so unkind to myself. I don't deserve that. No one does. Then I try looking at myself with new eyes and from a new angle that is filled with compassion, courage, and curiosity. When I do, I can lighten up, give myself some grace, and find the insight, grounding, and inspiration I need.

So, Gentle Reader, let Betsy's words and direction light your way. Imagine yourself whole, happy, and fulfilled. Use the wisdom and guidance in the pages that follow to know yourself better and become who you were really meant to be.

- What would you call yourself?
- Who are your allies?
- What are the beliefs that serve you, and which ones get in your way?

Our world needs more people who fully believe in themselves, people who are creating their dreams and creating ecosystems around them that are self-affirming and affirming of the people and communities that are important to them.

I hope you will begin today, knowing that you are part of our tribe and that Betsy and I are already your champions.

With warmest regards,
Lisa G. Carreño
President & CEO
United Way of the Wine Country

Lisa G. Carreño has been an attorney and nonprofit and community leader on both the east and the west coasts for over three decades. Her professional and community work has focused on social justice, family violence prevention, LGBTQI and immigrant rights, and access to higher education. After six years as the Regional Director for 10,000 Degrees in Sonoma County, Lisa joined United Way of the Wine Country as its President and CEO in August of 2018. She serves on the Boards of Directors of the Community Foundation Sonoma County, Los Cien Sonoma County, Forget Me Not Farm Children's Services, and the Rebuild North Bay Foundation. Lisa lives in Sonoma County with her wife, Lorene Irizary. Their three sons and daughters-in-law have blessed them with eight awesome grandchildren.

Introduction—My Why!

"I am uncomfortable with being comfortable," said Betsy to her executive coach.

Having accomplished many of my dreams and achieved much success in my 59 years on the planet, there is still so much for me to discover about what I don't know. If I am expected to slow down my desire to break through barriers, especially the ones I create for myself, then it's time to pack it in. The time had come to tell my story, which happens to be similar to what many of us have encountered over the span of a fruitful career. I have finally reached a time where I feel such pride for the woman I have become. There are no more reasons to hide or hold back. Life experiences have a way of sending those soulful messages that the time is now to lead brilliantly, regardless of the labels I have lived with throughout my time on the earth. My hope is to nudge you along on this journey and to help you remove the walls to embrace every part of your being.

"Shake It Off!" yelled my high school coach. Any athlete will tell you how important it is to shake off a bad play, regroup, and sprint to winning the next point. All of this miraculous action happens in seconds. And we do it over and over again. So, I carried those three words with me through business, marriage—and life. When Taylor Swift penned the song "Shake It Off," I chuckled because these three words have been ingrained in me for over 40 years, along with "I'm not enough," "Women are second," "Gays are fruitcakes," "Lesbians are dykes," and I can keep going.

Everywhere we turn, a new label pops up for a human category. Some labels serve as a badge of honor while others open deep wounds. We are in a divided world driven by labels as we passionately attempt to melt away the lines that cause hatred. Yet, here we are, battling other countries and each other as we find a label that brings some sort of peace. As a gay woman in leadership roles, I have lived a career of dodging the bullets of hate and discrimination as I nurtured a successful career as a business owner. Today, even with all the strides we have made in a diverse business environment, we still battle through the judgments and harm that come with being anything other than a Caucasian male. If you sense some frustration in my voice, you're right. After 35 years in the workforce and overcoming multiple obstacles to get to where I am, I'm a little tired of the extensive efforts put forth by myself and my diverse colleagues to then see a door quickly open for white males. Sorry, guys, I have to call it out. Sadly, the double discrimination still occurs in the LGBTQ community. As a woman or person of color, we still must push through harder to overcome discrimination. And, on a regular basis, I am honored to shake it off and burst through another obstacle. It has made me a better woman, wife, parent, and leader.

We have so many unconscious labels that flow through our minds and, to tell the truth, even the best of us have thoughts cross our mind that are best left unsaid. Some we can shake off and some we can't. Here are a few:

Men in general	Are womanizers. #metoo
White male:	He must be a Republican who voted for …
She's in leadership:	Who did she sleep with to get there? She must be a bitch.
Person of diversity:	They are successful because they receive "entitled" certifications (as though we are stealing something).

LGBTQ female:	She hates men. She hasn't met the right guy.
Introvert:	Poor wallflower, don't put them in front of a client!
Activist:	Must be one of those left-wing radical troublemakers (and by the way, I'm one of the people making good trouble—Rest in Peace, John Lewis).

And on and on with regard to age, height, weight, ethnicity, social class, etc. Within groups we have more labels and the list keeps growing.

When I look at the labels the universe gave to me, I learned so many lessons which, at times, broke my heart yet blessed me with incredible pride and strength. I am a wife and a mom to my wife's beautiful son and daughter. Matt and Carolyn teach and remind me about unconditional love, which was a quality missing from my own mother. I'm a grandmother to two granddaughters and one grandson. They call forth in me the simplicity of fun and how hugs and love are amazing gifts. Notice, I didn't use the terms *stepmom* or *stepgrandmother?* We'll talk about those icky labels later.

I'm certainly resilient, with a splash of fire that developed over years of being silent and compliant. With a courageous voice acquired from being pushed down for so long, I speak up for myself and for those in communities who need an advocate. As I learned to live with my labels and shake off the crap that came with them, I also acquired dysfunctional labels along the way. Being a proud recovering alcoholic—once I decided to acknowledge my addiction—for me is a badge of courage and honor. Alcohol numbed the feelings I carried about the walls I had to break through, but now I see the world from a different view, and it is far more beautiful.

As we wear our labels and either shake them off or embrace them, take a look at where privilege enters into our lives. Recently,

I was part of a group of LGBTQ leaders from around the world coming from all walks of life. As we went around the room to speak about our privileged backgrounds, I reflected on being a Caucasian woman with bachelors and master's degrees. I'm a successful entrepreneur. I have healthcare that I can afford, daily access to clean water, a nice home, a nice car, a happy marriage, a wonderful family, and I come from a respected family of origin. The label of privilege encompasses a large bucket of categories that many of us may take for granted or don't acknowledge. I am grateful for some of these liberties that I was born into and I give my all to use my influence to give voice to those who are not heard. And I ask all of you to see how you can use your privilege to make a positive impact in your work. There is nothing wrong with some of the positive labels we wear, it is how we wear them in the world that guides us in how we lead, love, and live.

Labels can make you stronger or weak; it just depends how you want to approach your life's circumstances. Nothing really "makes" you feel anything; it is all how we approach the experience. I chose to transform my labels into strength and empowerment with a dash of "knock it off." As you read about my journey, I hope you will discover the fire in your belly and wear your labels with pride. There will be a few times where my language will be passionate. If that makes you feel uncomfortable, shake it off and keep reading!!

I. THE JOURNEY

My Entrepreneurial Birth

To strive, to seek and not to yield.

—Alfred Tennyson

I first found this quote in high school and I've been riveted by it ever since. Somehow, early on, the universe was sending me a message that my life would be about striving, seeking, and not yielding when something was that important to me. When I look back, all the signs were there of what was ahead on my journey.

My family roots included small business owners on both sides of my family. My great grandparents and grandparents started a general store, grocery store, tavern, and garbage company. If you're thinking it, no, the *Sopranos* was not written about my family!! All the stories told to me about relatives of years past are consistent in that all of them were humble and hardworking, providing for their families local and abroad. Fervent savers, there was always plenty of food on the table, even when times were tough. Family and good food made the hard times easier to bear and that's pretty much the same mantra for my life today.

I am not a guru of any kind except for being the guru of myself and only myself. And that is more than enough. There are lots of self-proclaimed gurus out there who talk a lot of smack without being accountable for their blunders. Keep those people at a distance and pay close attention to see if their actions line up with their words. After much sweat, I have learned that if it doesn't have my name on it, I am not going to fix it unless it's an urgent matter or my wife and kids are in harm's way. Needless to say, I have way more energy and time when I stop rescuing people. We all get to claim, or not claim, the many layers of our individual journey, but it's not my work to take on others' journeys anymore. My journey keeps me plenty busy and I am sure you are way busy, too.

I started my company at 28, after a successful career working for a national recruiting company. At that time in my life, I was confident enough in my skills to branch out on my own. Working out of my house wasn't an option because structure was important for me to hit the ground running. I found an adorable basement office in a Baltimore City brownstone, hunted down really good deals on furniture and equipment, and the newest Executive Search firm in Baltimore was born!! It was a cold winter day in February, and I put on my favorite suit, best winter coat, and big-brimmed hat that clearly stated I had arrived. Into the front door I went, straight to my desk where I planned my day and picked up the phone to make my first cold call as CEO. I was proud and determined.

Within a week, we had our first orders from trusted colleagues and new businesses who liked what we had to say on the first call. In 1990, email was not the preferred mode of communication, so whatever message we left combined with a well-delivered introductory phone call, was the key to getting in the door. I came up with creative drop-offs to perspective clients that often got noticed. We had to stand out from the large competitors and, surprisingly, female managers were very responsive to my calls and often thrilled to give a woman-owned business a chance. For me, that open door came with a lot of pressure to over deliver, and I worked around the clock to seek out the best candidates to present to our clients. The first year started off encouragingly until the economy started to shrink.

It was a challenging time, but that didn't stop me, even when my old boss drove from New Jersey to woo me back to his company. I was flattered but told him that I now had a taste of entrepreneurship; I couldn't see myself going back to corporate. At the time, I wasn't set up to do temporary staffing because I didn't have a line of credit to support the business. Bankers back then were jerks when it came to giving money to women. We have successfully blown the lid off those idiots and we don't see as much of that behavior anymore, though it still exists.

A large Maryland corporation called me to provide temporary accounting staff to them because they were not happy with their current supplier. Given that I didn't supply temporary services at that time, I gave her the name and phone number of a competitor who did. She was surprised that I was willing to make the referral but, to me, that is good business. And if it worked for Macy's in *Miracle on 34th Street*, it seemed like the right thing to do. Lo and behold, a month went by and the client called me again and said she needed me to get in the temp business fast because she was not finding good service. We won her over on the executive search side and she wanted to be treated with the same level of customer service but couldn't find it elsewhere.

I did my research and found a company to handle the back-office process and fund the payroll. Back then, they were referred to as a "factoring" company. It's amazing what I pulled out of my hat when given the chance to grow the business. I secured it in a few weeks and began serving their temporary accounting staffing needs. This particular company was a long-standing high-volume client for 12 years until they went national and had to select large staffing companies causing myself and many small businesses to lose the account. I learned a big lesson early on to diversify our client base in order to minimize our economic vulnerability. Cash flow has a way of testing one's strategic thinking and resolve!!

Reading about other small business owners helped me through my most challenging times. Seeking counsel from others who overcame adversity guided me to reframe my obstacles and face them head on. I would spend hours at bookstores sitting on the floor surrounded by business books in search of the roadmap over my current hurdle. Those blocks of quiet time were—and continue to be—when I discover necessary wisdom for change.

What compelled me to write this book? After those bookstore jaunts over many years, I concluded that there are far fewer business books written by women. We are rapidly changing that, but since we now come in many shapes, colors, and backgrounds, I still think we need to see more women on the bookshelves telling our stories. We juggle businesses, families, and aging parents, and somewhere in that full life is often little time for self. Women can only grow more by sharing our journeys on the road to success, whatever that may look like for each one of us. We have an opportunity to shape the young generations of up-and-coming businesswomen and, with the state of the world, we need to bring forth more of our gifts in order to heal the pain of today's leadership styles. Sounds like that old "Super Woman" label. We have to be superheroes to keep up with our long list of responsibilities. And we do it!

I've come to learn that many of us approach leadership as a result of our upbringing. I grew up in a family where perception was everything and secrets were tightly held. I carried that into my professional life until I discovered my own truths—through many years of inner work. And it was a huge weight I carried for many years. One day, the switch flipped and I began openly sharing my struggles. Freedom became my friend. For the first time, the labels I ran from empowered me. I no longer hid from being openly gay but rather claimed my place as a lesbian business owner. In 2015, I was proud to call myself a recovering alcoholic because the alternative brought me a lot of sadness. And I am very much a powerful and outspoken woman because I won't accept crumbs any longer. If my passion makes another uncomfortable, it's not my issue to fix.

At age 59, I can joyfully say that I have so many wonderful experiences under my belt from which to draw upon for these pages. Some are heartbreaking and others triumphant. But all of them have truly shaped who I am in every facet of my life. I have had incredible teachers along the way—sometimes our best teachers are the ones who hurt us the most, including family and business partners.

I hope that what you read will propel you to take your life to a new level, like starting a new career, maybe opening your own business, facing/overcoming an addiction, or perhaps standing up to a bully in your life. Whatever it is, I truly hope you are on the path of happiness and inner peace. If the words, at the very least, make you pause and perhaps instill different messages to your daughter(s), then that's awesome. Remember, our millennials are our future leaders and, from where I sit, they have the grit to clean up our fragmented world. They embrace diversity as the norm, and I love their fearlessness to stand up to the status quo to say, "NO MORE!!" When young people stand at the podium and command our attention, we have to pass the torch. So, let them learn from our victories and mistakes.

Today, I am a successful business owner who has ridden the multitude of roller coasters that come with having a 30-year-old company. AdNet survived four economic downturns and survived each time because of dedicated employees, wisdom, and a heck of a lot of prayer. I have started new ventures, took on business partners, transitioned out business partners, and, through it all, managed to discover who I am amid the chaos called life. Business is fascinating and it is my art. I love immersing myself in a transaction and figuring out ways to have all parties win.

Surrounding myself with talented and honest people helps me to make solid decisions. If you don't have a good support system, write down where you want to see yourself, look at the areas where you feel less strong, and find people whom you trust and respect to fill your gaps. Little did I know that the roller coasters in business would sometimes resemble the roller coasters I would witness in my own family.

One of my many lessons I learned along the way was to surround yourself with people who are more talented in the areas where you are weak. That has helped me to create and sustain a successful company, team, and life. Each person on the team brings different gifts that, together, complement each other. At a recent company retreat, words that were shared to describe each other were *grounded, integrity, visionary, driven, dedicated, bright light* ... and I could go on forever. Since I took back sole ownership of AdNet in 2012, the culture has attracted amazing talent with beautiful hearts. The business model evolved since the 2008 recession where I outsourced several departments, which allowed me to spend more time on critical parts rather than managing multiple people. Our CFO is offsite, and she is gifted in putting numbers together that allow me to look at all parts of a business equation to make the best choices to propel the company forward. You must have a solid financial person in your company because the numbers tell the truth. Doesn't the truth set us free? That mantra works in one's business and personal life when you pay attention.

Remember the demise of Enron in 2001? That event also brought Arthur Anderson, one of the Big 5 CPA firms (as a result, is now the Big 4), to its knees because of illegal financial reporting, thus building a smoke screen to the outside and not only toppling a major corporation, but destroying retirement accounts for innocent hardworking people working inside Enron as well as those who were guided to include Enron in retirement portfolios. Let's not forget Bernie Madoff's Ponzi scheme in 2008, which caused further carnage within the financial world and innocent people's lives. Hmmm ... as we read about the level of greed that caused the severe financial wreckage, we see a theme of Caucasian men at the helm of the sinking ships. This is exactly why the feminine leadership label I wear so proudly propels me to call out this duplicitous behavior and ask fellow female businesswomen and my male counterparts with a conscience—and there are many—to change the vile practices of the greedy and bullying leaders who we are all subjected to on a daily basis.

I have an executive coach who calls me on my stuff and lovingly challenges me to take myself to the next level. What I adore about her is that her style is firm and loving, which supports me toward accelerated growth. A coach in my past life—and it was during a chapter of my life that I have since burned—was a bully who didn't practice the miles of advice that were dispensed. And God forbid I challenged "Beulah," (*the term my wife and I use to describe the negative people in our life*) I might as well have run for the hills. That was a time in my life when I was confident at the beginning of the coaching relationship but, like chipping away at an iceberg, allowed myself to be dumbed down and squelched. Sad to say, I allowed instances of emotional abuse in my own career. And I bet there are many business partnerships where this occurs, but we are ashamed to talk about it. Maybe if we start exposing abusive business relationships the behavior will stop. I faced several Beulahs, and the interesting darned truth is that Beulahs are always lurking in the world to ride on your coattails because they really aren't confident enough to make their own success. They come in all shapes and sizes and show up in all parts of our lives. The majestic part of the journey was finding my voice, kicking the Beulahs to the curb, and creating a life that is driven by passion and integrity. Trust your intuition!!

The life-changing events that helped to transform my life were the loss of my brother Tommy (Fr. Tom, a Roman Catholic priest) in January 2011 and my brother Jack in June of 2013. I had such close relationships with both and they were wonderful men who protected, advised, and loved me through whatever came my way. They were unconditional when my mother was conditional. My brothers and I were cut from similar molds, possessing sensitive sides as we held leadership roles in our communities. Both died alone of heart attacks. Yup, they had huge hearts giving to whoever needed help and, in the end, their devotion wore them out. They loved my wife like a sister, unconditionally. Tommy was the first person I came out to in 1982 and he held fast to his promise that his love for me was the same no matter who I loved. He also warned me that being gay in our family would be hard and he was so right!! Jack was the first family member I told when Susan and I decided to get married and he was so happy to finally call her his sister-in-law. Both men were so kind and they were my heroes. Crap, I'm down two loving heroes. They both represented the wonderful traits that I believe we need more from men and were not aggressive, chest-thumping bullies. Unfortunately, both never lived to see me marry Susan.

My life drastically changed in two phases after each loss. I found my voice again after Tommy's death and cleared out people from my life who were eternal takers and hypocrites. Jack's death forced me to take an inventory of my physical health, pay more attention to my well-being, and give up the demon called alcohol. And, while my heart will forever bear a huge hole once filled by their physical presence, I am more of a whole human being after having woken up to life by the loss of them. They gave me the gift of life again and that has propelled me to share with you how, at any point, we can wake up to embrace how beautiful our lives are. It is never too late to dream big and give back.

My hope here is that, through my hard knocks and my gentle wins, you say, "Hmmm, who and what is in my way of having my dreams come true?"

SHAKE IT OFF: *I'm a fan of Pro and Con lists, which I use all the time to guide people and myself to solid personal and business decisions.*

I want you to write a Pro and Con list of people in your life who make you feel good and the ones who are high-maintenance and/or toxic. You may find that the things that weigh heavy on your heart are from the people you love or, at least, the ones who always promised to love or protect you the most. You owe it to yourself to write an unfiltered list of people who are about as pleasant as a boil on your butt. If they give you angst, write down their name. If they suck the life out the room or your space, write down their name. As you look at the people on the Pro list, make sure there are more people who fill you up than the Beulahs who tear you down. Might be time to clear out the people-clutter in your life.

Where It Began

Success is falling nine times and getting up ten.

—Jon Bon Jovi

I am a Jersey Girl, the youngest of five in a Roman Catholic, white-collar, middle-class family. To the outside, we appeared prominent, a perception my mother worked hard to keep up even when her bank balance was low and credit card debt high. My parents raised us with the mindset that family and God were first. Everything we did was around church activities. Given our age range of 15 years between the oldest and the youngest, someone was either graduating from school, being Confirmed, or receiving First Holy Communion. Every special occasion was followed by an amazing meal prepared by my mother and grandmother. There was a lot of laughter, many people around the table, Italian food better than any restaurant I have gone to—even now, and let's not leave out the alcohol. It was always present, always flowing, and often the evening would end with my grandfather passed out in a chair after way too much scotch. I vividly remember cleaning the table, picking up his glass, and smelling the scotch. That smell still brings me back to the unpleasant memories of his alcohol-driven bombastic behavior. He was a hardworking man and a good man. Pop never raised a hand to anyone, he just got louder and louder the more he drank. Being very sensitive as a kid, I stayed clear of him because his bellowing was unsettling. Pop was my first exposure to a bully. When he chose his target to pick on, the bantering started off funny but ended up being inappropriate followed by many expletives. I remember putting my head on my mom's lap under the dining room table, so I didn't have to listen to him. As I went off to high school, it didn't seem to bother me as much. In 1978, he had an accident on a construction site that weakened his heart and softened his behaviors because he was physically weaker and drank much less alcohol. From that point on, a softer demeanor emerged. I enjoyed Pop more when he was gentler. Unfortunately, he passed away in 1982 from heart failure. My greatest sadness in his death was seeing my grandmother's sadness in adjusting to the loss of her soul mate.

As I got older, I spent a lot more time at my grandmother's house to keep her company. She was very strong and, as long as her family was close by, the world was wonderful in her eyes. There was something about her outlook on life that is still ingrained in my being. Nan was just plain happy; no pomp and circumstance was needed. She still had family picnics at her house and her smiling face was ever present on vacations and family gatherings. Sunday meals with my Nan felt like a holiday. She made my heart so genuinely happy and there was never strife, anger, or conditional love in her eyes. Nan loved all of us equally and there was no such thing as having to measure up to her standards. Whatever made us happy made her happy. My mother preferred the role of rule maker, unlike Nan, who was our playmate and protector. Just thinking about her makes my heart smile. I pray that as our new grandson grows and our granddaughters become adults, I bring them the joy my Nan gifted to me.

Each one of us brought our own individuality into the family system, yet that didn't impact Nan's love for any of us. My sister and I didn't have traditional "over the top, I can outdo you" type of Italian weddings, which burned my mother on some level because it was always about perception for my mother. It had to look impressive. My mother never got to see her daughters marry because of her disapproval of our choices. In retrospect, with the way she marginalized us, our mother didn't deserve the honor. If I sound a smidge bitter, it is because there are some residual sad feelings, given I dutifully showed up with a big smile on my face for every other family wedding.

Nan was the anchor that kept the teetering boat on course. My mother was on her own to raise us and get us settled into our lives and, frankly, my mother was not at her best during a crisis. We all prefer that life is smooth but aside from my mother's numerous attempts to control our life choices, she was also creating the disruption. I learned a lot about navigating turbulent business climates by the roller coaster of my mother's moods. Some days being in her presence was like walking on eggshells while other days it was smooth as silk. Through it all, my love for her was unconditional. But that's life and sometimes you have to shake it off and keep going.

I learned through my grandmother and mother to take care of myself, not because they neglected me. Just the opposite—my mother was smothering and I watched Nan keep both my grandfather and mother in their places. My grandmother was often aggravated by and sometimes would cry from my grandfather's insults, which only happened while he was drinking and showing off at a family gathering. But make no mistake, she held her own. One vivid memory is from when, after a Sunday meal, Pop was spouting his jokes and insulted my grandmother and told her to go back to the kitchen. With the aim of a professional ball player, she hurled an egg from the kitchen with such force that it hit him right on top of his bald head. Nan was not having that behavior anymore. Pop was shocked, stopped, and started to laugh, followed by his version of an apology. While he had the loudest voice, she clearly ran the household and held the line. He respected Nan because she stood up for herself. At a young age, I observed that it was evident their marriage was a partnership and they supported each other. Though they had the traditional husband and wife roles, my grandmother was independent with an equal voice.

I'm grateful to have learned early lessons of feminine self-confidence from my grandmother. Nan had this incredible optimism about her. She only had an eighth-grade education, yet she possessed wisdom that outranked any scholar. Born in Italy, Nan immigrated to America via Ellis Island as a child. Though her ethnicity was Italian, she never had an interest to return to Italy. Nan was a proud American Democrat!! I rarely saw my grandmother frown nor experienced her to be negative in any way. She loved simple things and loved her family through and through. We all ran to Nan when our mother was being difficult. There would always be a pep talk on "that's your mother" and a reminder that she was our mother and to show her respect. That advice held fast throughout my life and, to this day, showing respect to my elders is paramount, even as I am moving into an elder role, myself. I can't quite figure out what happens in the younger generations where our seniors are put aside, since I was mesmerized by the wisdom taught by those who came before me. Kids today just don't go out of their way for the elders. Somewhere down the road there will be a negative impact through the next generations. I'm just appreciative that I grew up showing respect for my elders and feeling loved in return.

Throughout my career, I have often heard, "You are so positive or an eternal optimist," as though it were a disease. Darn right I am. The alternatives of negativity just take people down and make navigating through business like walking through quicksand. I love that my grandmother's optimism shaped me because my mother was a "Fearful Fanny." Nan's positive outlook on life was the perfect balance for me to fend off my mother's negativity.

My grandmother had my grandfather take her to the roller rink when she was in her thirties, so she could learn how to skate. She would put on the skates and wheel herself along the railing until she had the courage to let go and skate among the oncoming crowd. Wouldn't you know it, she learned on her own, after many falls, but she freaking mastered it. When my mother watched me teach myself to rollerblade at age 34 was when she shared with me this story. "You are just like your grandmother," she would say. Yep, I am, thank God!! I wanted to master rollerblading and took myself outside, skating around and around a parking lot until I had it down pat. Nan was the one who came on all the amusement park rides with us on summer vacation. My mom said Nan would look green after, but she went anyway just to be with us. The waves of the Jersey Shore never held back the woman who didn't know how to swim. Her wisdom had her swim with my brothers close by as she held onto the thick rope that went from the shore to the buoy way out in the surf. It was clearly her love of us that had her overcome these fears. Nan learned how to drive in her fifties because she wanted to pick up the grandkids while Pop was working. It was her lead foot that I inherited!! This five-foot Italian woman with minimal formal education was my mentor. And she loved me regardless of who I loved. I learned unconditional love through Nan and continue to learn through my wife and kids, who give of themselves freely when they see anyone in need.

On the other end of the spectrum was my mom who was/is also a strong woman in a survival sort of way. I witnessed her swing from courage to cowardice back to courage and over again throughout the course of my life. After my father died in a car crash when I was six, my mother took on being the head of the household putting the needs of her family at the top of the list. Every morning my mom headed off to 6:30 mass to pray for strength and to quiet her mind. She did that a few hours after she was notified of my father's death, as though nothing had happened. Funny thing is, while I thought her ritual was obsessive in my youth, I now periodically attend morning mass before I head to the office. My mother also hid behind her church-going motherly label. She never missed church and she held fast to the Ten Commandments, which I totally get. Yet, when the behavior outside of church does not match the words preached from the pulpit, that is when I challenge religious teachings in general.

You don't get to say your prayers each week and put your fat envelope in the collection basket only to verbally or physically be abusive outside of those sacred walls. I have seen this behavior all my life from people who hold on tightly to the dogma of the Catholic Church and I have seen so much hypocritical behavior come out of the church I was ordered to attend. It didn't take long for me to see the inconsistencies in what I was told to believe and what I saw. Hell broke loose when I questioned it as a teenager. The wrath of my mother in that conversation was enough to have me never question it again until many years later. And, in the end, my journey for truth was stronger than her rules.

As the years wore on, my mother used passive aggressive manipulation as part of her survival skills. It became more evident to me in my adult years as I would have conversations with my brothers and sister to better understand our family dynamics. My mom never held back her opinion, which usually resulted in a "you can do better" or letting me know it was never enough. Those themes drove all five of us to strive to be highly respected and accomplished in our careers. In some strange way, my mother's relentless push probably saved us all because having had our family dismantled so tragically with the death of my father could have sent any of us into a downward spiral. As a result, my parents produced a gifted educator, banker, priest, business executive, and entrepreneur. Not too shabby!!

As I matured—and still to this day—I have thought about events in life where my mom worked her dysfunction. We were all targets of her dismay. I think the only sibling who was "perfect" was my brother Fr. Tom. We have all paid a lot of prices for her behavior, yet through it all, there is an unconditional love that we have toward our mother.

I am so grateful that I had the courage to move away at age 25. I was far enough to have my own life yet close enough to still be in arm's reach of painful dysfunction. None of what went on in our family is unusual, as every family has their warts. It is how you treat the warts that is the difference between living with joy or falling victim to your circumstances. It took me a lot of years to reach that point of joy and I hope through the journey that I share, you will be able to reach that point sooner than later. Our history is part of our fiber and, while it's not wise to hold tight to our history, it can also be a reminder of behaviors that are useful and harmful. I consider my history a Geiger counter to alert me to steer away from toxic situations.

Despite everything, there were buckets of happy memories with my mom. My mom has so many loving parts and she made my childhood very happy during a time that could have pointed me toward doom. My mom didn't date, so I became her companion for exploring culture. Memories are vivid of being eight to twelve and dressing up, often in dresses she sewed for me, and going to the Metropolitan Opera in New York City. As a kid, I saw *La Bohème, La Traviata*, and *Madame Butterfly*. She still reminds of how I would jump out of my seat clapping and smiling. I remember looking up at her smiling and watching joy beam from her face. During those years, we were best friends and she was my everything. We went to the movies all the time and, with my love of Barbara Streisand and Liza Minnelli, I managed to convince her that it was okay for me to see the PG and R movies as long as I promised to close my eyes during inappropriate scenes. Once in a while, her hand covered my eyes and I was so happy to be at the movies devouring popcorn with her, that I didn't mind when she had to do her mom thing. Every birthday there was a beautifully wrapped Barbra Streisand album waiting for me until she taught me to save my money to make my own purchases.

My childhood friends still remind me of the car trips where the station wagon would be filled as she took us to various amusement parks. Going to Catholic school came with getting out for a half day on Wednesdays for teachers' in-service day. Mom would pick me up and off we would go to Lord & Taylor to shop and have an early dinner at their restaurant. I always felt so special when she would order us something different to try along with a pot of tea. We didn't have a lot of money, but my mom knew how to stretch a dollar and we always had a budget of what we could spend when we went out together. Helen Reddy's song "You and Me Against the World" still brings tears to my eyes because we would sing it together whenever it came on the radio. Mom was my hero and I felt how much she loved me. Life with her was perfect until I fought for my sexuality. At age eight or nine, I clearly remember singing "I Gotta Be Me," by Sammy Davis, Jr., at the top of my lungs. Perhaps, early on, the universe was preparing me for what was to come.

Being part of my family dynamic taught me at an early age that being strong and assertive would get me to where I wanted to go. If I didn't speak up, no one was going to do it for me. If I didn't quickly reach for a second helping before my brothers reached for their third, I wasn't going to get any. Mom was committed to us all turning out well and being very concerned about outside perception. She worked hard to make sure we were had good educations, good jobs, and respect in our community. We all gave her a run for her money in our different ways. Looking back, I'm glad that we maintained our individuality and ultimately lived life the way we wanted. In her eyes, it was not the "perfect path," but nonetheless, we all did what we wanted. Sure, there were consequences, but we took our lumps from her and moved on. I only recall one spanking at my mother's hands. I was eight and, on a summer morning as my mother was reading the newspaper, I remember clear as day, "Mommy, I am going over to a friend's house (which was around the corner)." I was gone for a while and not within ear-shot of her back-porch yell. Apparently, she got scared and came looking for me. When she saw me around the corner playing, she ordered me into the car. I didn't think anything was wrong because I had told her where I was going when I left the house. Her "okay" response was permission to go. Well, when a mother isn't fully listening, an important detail like my location for playing is not heard. We get home and I followed her inside, still unaware of her anger until she picked me up, put me over the ottoman, and proceeded to give me the spanking of all spankings. While that was the only "beating" I ever received from her, I cried my eyes out because I had followed her rules, but she was not about admitting that she wasn't listening. I can count on one hand in my lifetime the number of times she has ever said, "I'm sorry." Watching my mother not be accountable for her mistakes impressed upon me that I didn't want to behave that way, so admitting my own mistakes came much easier. My wife will sometimes remind me to say I'm sorry and I'm a work in progress!!!

My mom was not one for showing much emotion, except her anger, so often we were left to deal with whatever was on our plate in our own way. Thank God we had grounded grandparents and solid friendships to talk through the challenges we all faced. I clearly remember Mom telling me that my dad had died and wasn't coming back. After the outburst of tears, she looked at all of us and out came the words, "You will show NO emotion. We will be strong for everyone else and cry after everyone goes home." Those words stuck with me for at least 20 years until I had the courage to go into therapy and found out that her request was not a healthy approach. Yet, it was what her generation was programmed to do. I kept my emotions held tight for many years. When I relearned how to release feelings, my life started to feel brighter.

High school was an absolute joy and I excelled at most things I touched with determination and a lot of elbow grease. I remember putting my sights on being a Senior Scholar Athlete as a sophomore and, with a lot of studying and practice, I achieved that goal. I was a kid who had to work hard to achieve success and that was okay with me because that made the victory all the sweeter. With my awards and scholarships in hand, I headed off to Catholic University in Washington, DC, with aspirations of becoming a pediatrician. I moved twice in my first semester before I found my core group of friends. Once I landed in Ryan Hall, I was home, and my soul felt settled with a group of women—who still are cherished friends. What I also found was total freedom from my mother's rules; no more curfews, no more checking in, and I did what I wanted when I wanted. It all sounds like heaven to an 18-year-old, but that experience brought out the rebel in me. I became an outstanding socializer, I drifted in and out of class when I felt like it and I barely cracked a book except for finals time. At that point, I was so far behind that the only way to survive was to cheat, but since that was not part of my fiber, I took my lumps and faced the music when the report card was mailed home while I was on Christmas break.

The mail came, and I tore open the envelope to see a whopping 0.8 GPA. Yes, you are reading that correctly, *point 8*. I did receive a B in English, but Calculus produced a D and Chemistry and Biology were big fat old F's!!! And I wanted to be a doctor. Well, smart ass, how was I going to talk myself out of this one? Being deathly afraid of The Warden, which was how I referred to my mother, I braced myself for the yelling and watched her shocked reaction. Some of the questions she shouted were: This must be a mistake? How could this happen to a National Honor Society student? How could you be so stupid? Are you a flunky? What losers are you hanging out with? All I could do was hang my head in shame and plead with her to let me go back and make it right. I was clearly on probation and would have to work my ass off to get out of trouble the next semester. She said she would give me her answer in the morning and went into her bedroom and slammed the door. My room was next to hers and I could hear her crying. That broke my heart. Being so much younger than my siblings, I witnessed various events in their lives that caused her distress and I promised myself not to cause her any pain as I got older. Promise broken, and that made me cry, so I crawled into bed and prayed that she would give me another chance.

Morning came, Mom went to church, and I patiently waited for her to return home. I was showered and dressed, just waiting, knowing deep down that I should have known better not to let my grades slip. When she walked in through the kitchen door, I sat there with much remorse and fear for the response that could come. Mom sat down and she said how disappointed she was and that I knew better than this. The questions came. Why didn't I ask my professors for help? Why didn't I call her to say that the courses were too hard and why didn't I give her a chance to help me? I didn't have much to say and couldn't come up with a logical reason other than in my head: I was having the time of my life!!! In retrospect, if I had told her my challenges with the classes, she would have helped me figure it out because my mother fiercely protected her cubs and she was smart as a whip. So, she gave me another chance. To stay at school, I had to bring my grades way up or else I had to come back home and go to the community college. That option was not possible for me because, now that I had a taste of life outside of Perth Amboy, I knew then that I was never coming back.

The rest of my college years were a time of discovery and finding my way. By my sophomore year, I realized that medical school was not going to be my path, so I moved toward business. I saw the favoritism toward men in getting ahead of the line for medical school and, at that time in my life, I didn't have the discipline to push through the maze of barriers. My political internship on Capitol Hill in my senior year was my favorite job because I had a taste of life on The Hill. I almost walked into Nancy Reagan, sat in the gallery during speeches by international leaders, and walked through the government buildings like I lived there. It was an incredible experience and I loved all the menial tasks that came my way. There were many political science students clawing for these jobs and I secured mine easily since Congressman Barney Dwyer had been good friends with my dad. My mom came in handy making a phone call when any of us needed a door opened. She never told me if she made the phone call but all I know is that when I walked in bearing the last name Cerulo, Mr. Dwyer welcomed me with open arms and started to cry as we talked about my dad. My dad was such a good man and left a huge imprint on so many people. Within 30 minutes, the job was mine. I managed to get away with "calling in sick" when the previous night of partying ended late. Once I graduated college, I instinctively knew that missing work was never an option, no matter the reason.

As I started on my career path, something inside told me that I wanted to make a name for myself without the help of my family. It was important to me that I entered a workplace where no one could care less about my last name. That motivated me and, in the end, took me on an adventurous journey where I could be my own person at every turn.

Many families of origin come with their own set of biases. Women are expected to act differently in business, which often we are groomed for as young girls. I'm not sure what prompted me to speak up for myself in business other than I would overhear my brothers talk about their work experiences. And I observed them get what they wanted, which passively taught me that when I speak up for myself, I will get what I want. When I felt successful with that approach, I tried it a few more times. It didn't always produce the outcome I wanted. At those points, I sought advice from business colleagues and friends for guidance.

When a goal meant a lot to me, I kept pressing on. There were times when the goal created conflict and sometimes, I caved into the fear that led to me giving up. As time passed, my intuition would scream loudly, to the point where I could no longer avoid the denial. Like a fighter in the ring, I would bandage my wounds, listen to wise guidance, and get back into the fight until I won. Looking back, I have achieved victory in business with bruises and exhaustion, yet the gut-wrenching journeys were often my best lessons.

Following the traditional path of college degree, marriage, then kids was not on my mind in my younger years, much to my mom's disappointment. Deep down, I never saw myself married to a man. It was one of those inner knowings that can't be explained. I wanted freedom to discover my newfound sexuality and prosper in a career, which was still unfolding in my early twenties. The 1980s were not a time to have children outside of pregnancy/ adoption unless there was a man at my side. Well, since that wasn't going to happen, I kind of closed the door to any chance of starting a family. Children need a parent who is fully present and, in my twenties and early thirties, that's not where my head was at. I loved my career and freedom.

When I met my wife in 1998, she had two teenagers and almost overnight I had my family. And I surely did not know how to manage teenagers with their own set of wishes and wants. There were many bumps along the way. Yet, as I step back looking at our life, we all chose each other. My kids often put themselves at the bottom of the list when it comes to loving and helping others unconditionally. I grew up in a conditional family where I would be considered perfect if I followed traditional expectations. My kids are nontraditional PERFECTION!! They teach me all about unconditional love in a way that makes the sun, moon, and stars line up.

I'm really blessed to have such a loving family at this stage in my life. When we are all together, I often am quiet, observing the ease and silliness we have together. There is no judgment. As my wife says, "We all love each other for who we are and for who we are not." That's family.

To anyone out there from a large "traditional" family, don't let them yank your chain to stay close to the nest. The rules favored boys and the girls were supposed to be the caretakers left behind to tend to the home duties. That behavior went on for decades for me and it was only when I became sober that I saw the dysfunctions so clearly. And, without any guilt, I learned how to speak up for myself and say no to what didn't feel fair. My life is much happier for it. And, believe me, it took a lot of courage to buck the family of origin system and I'll never look back.

SHAKE IF OFF: *Be your own person and follow your own compass. Your North Star is the brightest star you will ever see.*

Faith or Fluff?

Your beliefs don't make you a better person,
your behavior does.

—Sukhraj Dhillon

Though I grew up Catholic, I choose not to practice the religion. I am at peace with my decision to seek spirituality outside of practices I learned in my childhood. In business, I observe that people are more willing to speak about their faith when working in an environment that welcomes the conversation when it's appropriate. We are all flawed and when our flaws are mixed with our gifts, we are beautiful humans. Hearing a spiritual conversation gets my attention as I witness joy on the person's face when they speak about their practices. Since religion is a topic that can be risky to discuss, be mindful of when to have those conversations. If it can cause strife, don't engage.

Interestingly enough, today I find prayer as my greatest source of calm. I start off my mornings, pause throughout the day, and end the evening with prayers of thanks. Whenever I need to make an important decision, I ask the question clearly to God before I go to sleep and trust that when I awake, the answer will be clear. And it is always delivered. I'll be the last one to tell you who to believe in, but what I can attest to is that all the amazing people I respect and want to emulate have some type of spiritual practice that keeps them grounded. Now, I will tell you that there are some days when I am on rails with thoughts that strangle my serenity.

But every time I slow down my madness, sit still, and ask for what I need, calm is restored.

My relationship with God has allowed me to overcome intense challenges as well as provided me with sought-out answers. It comes down to the stillness needed to hear what your spiritual guide tells you. And the "guide" may show up differently for different people. So, don't judge another person if your beliefs are different. I pay attention to a person's words to see if their actions line up with their beliefs. It's the same in business. Look for consistent messages and direction that is aligned with your values. There are a lot of gurus out there claiming to have the "right" answer. Choose the practice that resonates within your soul.

A person with strong faith will tell you that a religious practice is the key to success, and some will tell you otherwise. Your faith is just that—YOUR faith. Follow your soul and, in my humblest opinion, when in doubt, look to the universe and your spiritual practices to guide you toward your success, whatever that may be. I am most successful when I take the time to be with God and express gratitude for the life I have been given.

One of my brothers was a devoted Catholic priest before a heart attack laid him to rest in 2011. I swear it was the laziness and egotistical fellow priests who drove him to his early grave. Some were power-hungry and, for the most part, lazy men who thought their collar meant they deserved special treatment ahead of the rest of humanity. Tommy never asked for leadership, he just naturally took charge and walked courageously through a multitude of challenges, even when the burden seemed too much to bear. But Tommy? Well, he was the real-deal priest, devoted to God, the message, and his congregations. Much of today's clergy have the meaning of service backward—they think their congregations are in service to them. We are here to serve together and build a prosperous community from the heart to the bricks and mortar in which people worship.

The message my brother, Fr. Tom, always impressed on me was that it didn't matter to him where I worshiped, as long as I held a strong faith in God. And that I do, and it's personal for me. I pray daily, I ask God for guidance, and especially find my center through meditation. Imagining myself sitting within nature and feeling one with God settles my soul and provides me with the guidance that I ask for as I start my day. Most of my important decisions came out of those quiet moments in prayer. And some days for me prayer is in the car on my way to a meeting. I can't always have my Buddha-like moments but one thing that has always been evident is that God accepts me however I am. Too bad the world is so conditional. Oh, we'll get to that chapter, too!!

SHAKE IT OFF: *Find yourself a daily practice that works for you. Be consistent, sit quietly, and ask the universe for what you need. Be ready to receive. As you explore your new practice, watch the behaviors of your teachers. If they don't practice what they preach, move on.*

Who Are YOU?

You are a very special person. There is only one like you in the whole world. There's never been anyone exactly like you before, and there will never be again. Only you. And people can like you exactly as you are.

—Fred Rogers

Enough of me ... let's talk about YOU!!! If you are reading this book, you are exploring insights on your road to successful leadership. I'm genuinely happy that you are yearning for new practices or minor fine-tuning to enhance your journey. Every day is filled with opportunity for change and improvement. And I evaluate those aspects in my own life daily. It's rigorous yet the exploration keeps me focused. Life is an ongoing journey.

Let's talk about where you are and the labels you are carrying, at this point in your life:

■ Working for a corporation and feeling the entrepreneurial itch
■ Have a business and want to kick it up a notch
■ Have a business and want to make it work for you
■ New in your career and want to make a difference through leadership
■ An established leader who wants your leadership to take on a different path

- None of the above and have had enough with diverse groups being targets of discrimination
- Your sexuality is rattling inside your soul and it's time to honor your truth

Wherever you are, no matter your age or circumstances, keep following your dream or create a new chapter. Know that you may need to shake off labels that no longer serve you or embrace labels to call forth your passion.

This can be challenging, since new labels seem to pop up daily via social media, which can be empowering and confusing all at the same time. I am a woman, first, who is pushing to see our gender treated and paid equally. Our female leadership label is one I wear with great pride. Women are gifted with heightened intuition and, when we use it fully, it is one of our premier qualities. Most great leaders will convey that the foundation of some of their best and worst experiences was based on the degree in which they/we listened to our intuition.

I love to talk about leadership and, through my public speaking, I find myself weaving in female leadership at every opportunity. We, as women, have walked through centuries of being second to our male counterparts because of the gender label. Let me be clear, most of my business mentors were men who I deeply respect. Through my journey, I have spoken out for women and pushed the younger generations to stand up against being pushed around by men in business. Think about it: Gender roles were taught by generations of parents. My parents' generation learned that women stayed home to raise kids, were the emotional foundation, managed the household, and were the strength behind their husbands. Men were—and in some relationships today still are—the financial providers, protectors, and fixers of everything broken. When the couple operates as a partnership, that model works beautifully, but there are some models where the woman is all those things yet is expected to be silent and in the background.

Fortunately, my grandmother and mother held their roles with much pride and were respected by my grandfather and father. They spoke up and, in a quiet way, really did run the roost. They taught me how to stand up for myself, even when the lesson came from standing up to my own mother. :)

We have read the history books about women's suffrage at the turn of the century. Women could not own real estate, women needed men to apply for loans, had no abortion rights, and had no equal pay—or should I say non-equal pay, since we are still earning considerably less than men. Woman are earning about 79 cents to a white man's dollar, with that number much less for women of color. It's baffling how some men can't understand why we are just plain done with their behaviors toward us and why we fight back against their ignorance. As a gender, we have been programmed to be second to men. Within diverse groups, the problem is worse, which is why we must keep speaking out. There were amazingly courageous women before me who opened the doors of opportunity, so I had the choice to be who I am today. And there are so many courageous women today like Oprah Winfrey, Michelle Obama, Sheryl Sandberg (COO of Facebook), Marillyn Hewson (CEO of Lockheed Martin), Ursula Burns (CEO of Xerox), Indra Nooyi (CEO of PepsiCo), as well as you and me, who are designing new opportunities for the generations to come. Growing up in the 1970s, I was mesmerized by New York City Congresswomen Bella Abzug and Shirley Chisholm. They represented courage and pushed back at the status quo. I dreamed of someday having the courage and influence to build communities that honored women; I'm here because I would not give up.

It's important for women to find our voices and use them wisely despite any label we wear. Let the label be your badge of honor to guide you over the hurdles of leadership. More and more women are saying "no more" to belittling behavior. And, the more we interrupt being demeaned, the more serious we will be taken and the stronger we become. I recently was waiting my turn to make a purchase when a man did his best to push ahead of me. Earlier in my life, I would have been polite and stepped back. I looked at him and calmly said, "You can wait patiently the same way I have." He was caught, stepped back, and didn't say another word. Be a leader, speak up, and take your place at the front of the line. How we show up in life is a reflection of our leadership style. There was a time I took a step back, but those days are long gone. Interestingly enough, I took my leadership to a powerful level after navigating a toxic business relationship with another female. Being a bully is NOT gender specific. A word of wisdom for those women who have a nasty edge in their leadership style that is disempowering: Don't be punitive to your team. Lead with courage and pride. Leave the attitude at home!!

Deep down inside, anyone who is reading this book is someone who wants to make a difference. We have stories to tell from all walks of life. You don't have to write a book, but you should share your story with other women. What we find is that there are quite a number of us out there wanting to be heard, wanting to be pushed to the front of the line, and ready to stop any behaviors from men or other women who make us feel small. We can shift the current misogynist mindset in the world by teaching our kids and grand-kids to treat everyone with the same respect. And, whatever you do, push back against any blowhard—male or female—who tries to hold you back. Remember, only YOU can hold YOU back.

So, who are you? Take some quiet time, grab a journal, and answer these questions. Let the words flow and don't worry what it looks like. This exercise is just for you. Here goes. Now be honest and let yourself dream.

■ What drives you?
■ What matters to you?
■ What are the things in your life that you want to change?
■ What do you like about your life?

- Is there a personal or professional relationship that is no longer serving you?
- What would your life look like if this person or behavior no longer had power over you?
- What is the worst that could happen if you changed this relationship?
- What do you think is holding you back from making this change?
- What are you most fearful of right now?
- On a scale of 1 to 10 with 10 being the best, how happy are you with your life?

As I said, let the words flow whether that is putting pen to paper or typing on a computer. Give yourself the freedom to feel these questions at your core. We can be afraid of the truth and still take steps to make necessary changes that can lead us to a 10 in happiness and/or success. When we have these two areas balanced in leadership, we are most effective. Our teams pay attention to our actions. It is important for us to know who we are as leaders and then model healthy behaviors. Did you notice the numerous labels here: *happiness*, *success*, *balance*, and *healthy*? These are labels to embrace. Take time to shake off sadness, failure, stress, and sickness, which make leadership an uphill battle.

Every day we walk through life may not yield the perfect 10, yet we have the power to create more 10s than we may have right now. That was my goal when I found my long-lost voice. I know some days life feels hard, but where I am at now, even after taking the lumps, I am more solidly living life at a 10 than I was before I turned 50.

Being young does not always mean more happiness. Yeah, sure, I had way more energy, slept better, and could burn the candle at both ends while still having mind-blowing results in my job. Today, I run a little slower and can't multitask at warp speed, but I am so much happier that I shed several skins of dysfunction in my life. I could only have come to this point when the pain became too much to bear. Abundant blessings have grown out of my wounds and I am grateful to be 59 with so many blessings rather than 47 and avoiding the truth.

As I inch closer toward my retirement years—which is a label on most newsletters that pop up in my email—I am NOT going to stop working. My work is meaningful. Retirement and age do not make us irrelevant. Don't ever attempt to put me out to pasture or you will surely lose your front teeth!!! Years of experience have broadened my wisdom. When it's time, this is a label we all need to embrace as we reframe our careers. I like my various work outlets. This means passing on the torch in one aspect of my life and having more time to touch more lives, more time to speak out for equality, and more time to make life a better place for our three grandchildren.

So, I ask you again, who are you? If you don't have a clear picture yet, what are you waiting for? Start your inquiry now because time is passing regardless of if you are clear or unclear. Might as well be clear. Life is a continuous process and journey that requires mindful attention and rigor when you want to achieve a certain result.

If you are effective in your job and not in your personal life, I challenge you to give that part of your life the same attention you give to your successful career. If your personal life is happy while your professional life is stressful, I challenge you to take a leap and put happiness before the paycheck. This can all be done with practice and that is what we will explore in the rest of this book. So, get comfortable wherever you are, put your feet up, and let's make life joyful. Because we all deserve it!!

SHAKE IT OFF: *If you want to truly know who you are in life, get really quiet, have a heart to heart with yourself, and listen. Shake off the noise and embrace the wisdom in your soul.*

Find Your Voice

You've got to tell the world how to treat you.
If the world tells you how you are going
to be treated, you are in big trouble ...

—James Baldwin

What does that mean for you? Where would you like to be more forthright with your opinion? What have you allowed to go unchallenged that makes you unsettled inside? Are you concerned about what others will think if you were to speak up when you experience an injustice? Do you think you'll be labeled a "bitch" if you stand up to anyone, especially a man? I bet if he stood up for his opinions, he would be viewed as a leader. But us, nope, we get labeled a bitch. Well, though I don't like the word because often it's used maliciously, I'll wear my bitch label proudly when used to refer to my leadership directness.

Don't even think you are going to squelch my opinion. If you even try to hold my business matters as less important as yours, I will fire you as a client. Funny thing is that when I have made the choice to stop a business relationship, it's been with mostly woman-owned companies. Periodically, I have experiences with some women business owners who act holier than thou, as though their time is far more important than mine. By comparison, I have experienced this with companies that are larger in revenue than AdNet. If you think I am going to have my staff or myself waste precious time running in circles, you've got another thing coming.

Take that behavior elsewhere because it's not welcome here. Interestingly enough, when my staff or I have spoken up to an aggressive male client, our level of respect has been elevated by leaps and bounds, to the point where we are now regarded as peers.

So, just to clarify, this is not a male-bashing book; this is an interruption to business and personal behaviors as well as challenging the labels that get in the way of achieving our very best. We spend time dodging idiots, holding back on wise feedback, and micromanaging our own words so we don't lose clients. In the end, we lose our self-respect. Our view of ourselves is far more important than stroking the ego of some high and mighty decision-maker. I have done business with the biggest self-absorbed, aggressive personalities and bigoted buttheads, which has provided my company with much financial success over the years. But, after I shed the "good girl" approach and told—with well-chosen words—both male and female bullies to stop their nonsense, the relationship became collaborative and easy.

And so, you know, women can be just as abusive as men. In business, they may show up as being on your side, and we would assume that because we are in a diverse category, wanting all to succeed. But I have found a few very successful women who will take what they can from other women to get ahead. True story: Inevitably, when I run into Tonya, a business owner who has a $20+ million company, she always attempts to bleed me for information. Perhaps the perception or label women bear is that we are expected to share information with whoever asks, whereas it is more common for a man not to share feelings in a "holding it close to the vest" practice. And that has always been acceptable. When I first entered into government contracting, I would share what I knew because there were several women business owners who graciously took me under their wing, and my style is to share information when I am asked for insights. After about the third interaction with Tonya probing for my secrets, the next time she asked, I looked at her and said, "Gee, Tonya, I don't know, what do you think?" Now, when I see her, I get compliments up and down for whatever she has read about me. But she is one of those "red flag" people who will now hear a generic response from me regarding what I know. It takes a few interactions to figure out who genuinely wants to share business or who would scratch out your eyeballs to get there first. Sometimes, using your voice also means smiling and moving on. You don't have to answer every question and you don't have to tell off everyone who doesn't act the way you want them to. Over the years, I have learned to be more mindful in giving away information or answering whatever question I am asked. Now I pause, listen, and choose to share my thoughts mindfully or not comment. In a business setting, it's best to be gracious, wise, and then move on. Please don't mistake graciousness for being a pushover. I can be gracious and firm at the same time as I pay close attention to watch if actions match words.

When busy professionals are in the middle of getting the extensive list of to-do's checked off, they/we/I can sometimes forget our human side. With the right words, a good jerk can turn into your best client. But if you keep accepting toxic behavior or "my time is more important than yours" behavior, you will continue to get back what you accept, which is a labor-intensive low-margin client. When you must constantly stroke their ego or go into a transaction in a constant state of angst, you will eventually lose money because your time is spent chasing when you could use that time nurturing positive business relationships. The clients who regard you as a partner give you the best return, even when you work your butt off. I prefer going above and beyond for a client I adore. And, above all, be genuine with your customer service approach.

Your voice is your best resource to design your success. Ask for what you want and need without fear of being labeled. The fear you may carry may be easier to overcome once you are aware of the feeling. This is the same with your spouse, your kids, your parents, and your siblings. I would have to say my hardest "client" has always been my mother. The only label she wanted me to wear was that of a heterosexual married female with kids. It was the heterosexual label that had us at odds most of my adult life. Other than that, my mom and I always had a close relationship, even when she was at her strictest. Looking back, I can appreciate the focus on structure and accomplishment in her mother-child expectations. Since my dad died when I was six, anything less than a strong parent could have sent me down a precarious road of poor grades and teenage trouble. Just to be clear, you can be a strong and present parent and your kid can still make poor choices. Back in the 1970s, there was no Internet influence or technology overload. My mother was both my influence as well as my overload, for which I am grateful.

I had a voice with my mother, even when she didn't want to hear it. She was clear when it was time to not be heard and I respected her authority. But I learned young how to dodge her rules. Being the youngest of five, I saw the challenges between her and my brothers and sister. I didn't buck the family pecking order, but I did watch actions carefully. I saw how my brothers got away with so much nonsense while my sister and I were held to a different standard. That always bothered me when my sister was called out for her choices and unfairly treated. My brothers did the usual guy things of average grades in school, complaints from teachers, getting drunk, fights, etc., yet my sister and I had excellent grades. I was promised a car for excellent grades in high school; my sister was promised a trip upon college graduation, but neither of us saw the rewards while my brothers received new cars. Totally unfair.

I started to push back at my mother after I went to college. At Catholic University, I discovered my identity outside of my Italian Catholic family filled with conditional rules. Voices were heard as I experienced political opinions that were not in my realm of thinking. I was exposed to protests, the Iran hostages' return to the United States, and having an opinion about presidential candidates not just because my family voted a certain way. There was no VOICE over me to study, which opened a new world for me to fill my time with whatever I wanted whether it was productive or not. Hearing about international cultures was so new for me. You mean there is life outside of being Italian??? I remember Carla, an Iranian woman who lived on my floor and cooked her native meals. Most of us had no clue about the smells that were coming from her room. We playfully teased her, and she always smiled graciously as we laughed together. She was such a sweetheart. There was acceptance as we all discovered life together.

My voice really took hold after I came out as a lesbian in 1982. I wasn't out in all aspects of my life. My sexuality was compartmentalized depending on the situation. The Career Betsy was very much straight while the Friend Betsy was very much gay. The Cerulo Betsy had to walk a fine line for fear of abuse. I wasn't 100% sure of when to be inside or outside the closet, but I knew that life looked like a field of beautiful flowers vibrant with color as I tapped into this side of my being. Oh, but my mother didn't want to hear any of it. I was as direct as I could be when she drove down to visit me for the weekend to talk. She wanted to understand what I was thinking and, as best as I could muster up the courage, I said, "I think I'm gay." I could see my mother's heart breaking and, having seen her cry over the years from disappointments with my siblings, I sure as hell did not want to be another reason a bite was taken out of her heart. She held onto the words "I think I'm gay," praying hard that this was a phase that would pass once I moved back home after the school year. All she would say was, "Just come home and we'll work this out." I really trusted her, but if coming home meant that I would end up in the usual youngest unmarried sibling role of being the caretaker and babysitter in the family who would be the old maid, loyal to her mother and brothers ... THAT AIN'T HAPPENING!! I would have rather slit my wrists than wear that blasted label. And that is truly what still is expected in many "traditional" families. The unmarried girl is the Cinderella without the prince or, in my case, the princess.

Finding my voice became a matter of survival as I embarked on finding my sexuality. It was never my intention to hurt my mom and it wasn't personal. It was who I was, and my soul was scream- ing. I had to defend my choices within my family. One relative took it upon themselves to push me around as though they had the final say in my life's choices. Those early days of experienc- ing rage stayed with me, even after sincere apologies years later. The memories remain, even with forgiveness. No one has a right to hit another person, especially when it's from friends or family who say they love you. From that point on, I remained on guard when I had interactions with anger mongers. Trust me, the leopard doesn't change its spots, which I encountered even in my fifties. This time around, my voice is nice and strong, and that leopard will lose every time. I have zero tolerance for bullies. They are held at a comfortable distance.

Let me ask you if there has been a time in your life when any of these things occurred:

- You felt a physical sensation when your voice was at its strongest?
- What did you experience?
- What was the outcome?
- Do you trust that voice?
- Have you lost your voice?
- Has anyone quieted your voice?

I bet if your voice has been squelched, you wish like hell it would come back. And it can. I promise you with every fiber in my body that once you regain your footing to open your vocal cords, your life will be set free. Your relationships will shift—some may fall off to make room for more loving people. Your workload will lighten as employees, teammates, and family members get to carry their workload. You see, when you do for others who are very capable to do for themselves, the only one who gets exhausted is YOU!! Stop the madness and say what you need and, if they say no, you get to make a choice. Can you live with keeping things at the status quo or do you have the courage to walk away? It might seem like you are losing something, but what you are gaining is time to do what you need for your own well-being.

Once my company received certification as an LGBT Enterprise in 2012, the logo was on every piece of marketing material. No matter what venue or audience, I proudly spoke about my LGBT certification. At a time when LGBT rights are at risk, politically, my voice at federal government events is clear and certain as I speak about all the company's certifications. If a prospective client is uncomfortable with the LGBT certification, then this is not the best customer for us to service. At this point in life, I am true to who I am and I challenge you to be true to yourself as well. Once you open that door and declare who you are—whoever that may be—you will never be able to be less than who you are. Corny as it sounds, the truth really does set us free.

I can very clearly remember the day I told my mother that Susan and I were married. After Marriage Equality became a Maryland law in 2013, we were talking and Mom forbade me to marry Susan while she was alive. Yeah, like this 52-year-old woman was going to be stopped from marrying the love of her life. So, against my better judgment, I didn't tell my mother. She was 89 and had just buried a second son, and I couldn't find the courage to tell her. Interestingly enough, around the time of my wedding, only my oldest nephew told me to be honest with her and tell her because I should not hide something so important in my life. If I could turn back time, I would have listened to him. In the summer of 2014, I went up to visit Mom with the sole purpose of sharing my happy news. I was tired of holding it back. I woke up in the morning ready to tell her. Then I decided to go out for a run. Run out my fear, I thought. I came back and made us breakfast. As we sat at the table, all I could think of was, that in the 10 seconds it would take me to share my HAPPY news, I would be free. I still sat there with my heart racing from fear. Then it came … my inner voice said, "Practice what you preach," and that was enough for me to keep my word with myself. "Ma, Susan and I were married last September on our fifteenth anniversary and I'm proud of it and I love her, and it was the happiest day of my life." I felt this huge weight lift from my shoulders. My next words, "You said last year that I couldn't marry her until after you died and my marriage is my choice. You married the love of your life and I deserve to do the same and I'm happy." At that moment, I was prepared to go pack my bags and head back to Maryland. She looked up and said, "Those sound like words I would say and I'm happy that you are happy. I have old-fashioned ways and I'm stuck in tradition, but I only want you to be happy. Sue is good to you and I see that. Does anyone else in the family know?" I replied, "Everyone knows." She laughed and said, "I'm still always the last to know everything." She held my hand and wished me happiness.

Geez, I had made this so hard for myself because of my fear. From that point forward, there were no more issues between us when it came to my marriage. Fast forward to 2021, my mom is in a nursing home with dementia and is wheelchair bound. Yet, whenever Susan and I come to visit her, Mom always says, "Hi Sue," without hesitation. And in every conversation, Mom asks me how Susan is … even with dementia, she knows how important Susan is in my life.

Unfortunately, our children and grandchildren were invisible to Mom. No matter how many times I talked about Matt and Carolyn, she would refer to them as my wife's family, not as mine. There was never an acknowledgement, EVER. No gifts exchanged, no congratulations for any milestone, not even a simple greeting card sent to them. We, as a family, were invisible, operating as an island, and separate from my family of origin. The concept of honoring my place as a parent, grandparent, and wife were denied unless I spoke up. My mother was not the only person in my family to hurt me that way. As I said before, there was a lot of hypocritical behavior in a family that was supposed to be grounded in our faith.

When I ponder the regrets in my life, the most passionate regret was that I did not fight hard enough to make a place for my wife and kids within the almighty Cerulo family persona that my mother created. That is my job as a parent and I failed them, my wife, and myself for not pushing back from the start and continuing to push until my kids were as important as the rest of my nieces and nephews. My kids came to New Jersey for my mother's 94th birthday party in 2018 and have never once been invited to family weddings. And I have been told several times that I can't bring them to events for whatever stupid reason. The last time those words were spoken, I fought with gusto and rage to make sure this never happened again. And the interaction rattled me for months because that type of fighting is toxic for me and not how I live my life. But I now will battle for my kids because they are my #1 family. The years of out of sight, out of mind with minimal effort by my family of origin wore me out, and I metaphorically released myself from hoping for anything more and allowed my ship to sail and stay happily anchored in Maryland with people who truly love me unconditionally, warts and all, with no rules. My kids deserve my unconditional loyalty. Those who hold my kids or my place in their life as insignificant don't have a place in my world anymore.

This is one of those personal experiences that I have had to shake off to embrace all of the goodness in both my personal and professional life. The heavy weight of conditional behavior from my family of origin weighed on my leadership style and I allowed it to keep me small. Once I released the angst, I felt reborn as a leader. No surprise that all within the same timeframe, I claimed a stronger me and rebranded my company. And I bet you will, too.

The whole notion of being labeled a stepparent evolved for me over time. We all walked through many happy and challenging times together well before Susan and I legally married in 2013. When Susan and I committed to each other as a couple in 1998, she asked me to embark on the role as co-parent, which also required careful steps. At that time, the kids were 18 and 19 and were making their own decisions. I would take my place in the background because Susan was their biological mother and our relationship was very new. Since stepparenting was not about taking a class and getting a grade, my lessons were by trial and error, and I made a pile of errors. My happiest early memory was standing next to my daughter as she gave birth to Alyssa. Susan felt faint during the delivery and had to sit down. I panicked and asked, "What do I do?" And from the couch came, "Tell her to breathe." I jumped into place and kept one eye on my daughter and one eye on the miracle that was coming into the world right before my eyes. I was in awe as my little Luli slowly entered the world with her first scream. I stayed close as the doctor guided Luli into the world and sutured Carolyn back together. Though I never had the yearning to be pregnant, at 37, I could bear witness to this beautiful miracle of our granddaughter's birth. And years later, I get to retell Luli the story of her first entrance into the light.

A number of years later, a good friend and I had a disagreement over planning a get-together. When I didn't agree with Marsha's opinion, her response was, "What would you know, you never had children." Those words were a kick in the gut. Folks don't EVER say these words to a stepparent!!!!!! The capacity for love is not only gifted to people who have conceived and birthed children. Love is love and there are plenty of us who discover solace and healing from people who are outside our DNA. Our "logical" family are the ones we choose and often fill the deep holes that our "biological" family of origin create.

As I have entered another phase of grandparenting, I am more sensitive to the subtleties of carrying the *step* label. I have been referred to as Susan's wife over being referred to our kids' mom. In being part of conversations of excitement over the birth of our new grandson, there were a couple of instances where women only acknowledged the pride Susan must feel even though I am standing there next to her. I know there is no intentional harm, but it is a subtle exclusion because I am not the birth mother. We all need to be mindful of the subtle biases that we have with labels. My gift here is that I am more conscious of inclusion with others who wear the step label. So, rather than standing by as though I don't exist, I gently move myself into the conversation where I feel included. These are innocent exclusions and it's up to me to change the conversation.

And it is up to each of us to use our voices to make positive change. There are certainly plenty of toxic voices out there, which is more reason to tap into our goodness to be heard. One positive voice leads to another positive voice, which continues to grow. It is up to us individually to set good examples by finding our courage to speak our truth. Once we begin this journey, our inner wisdom peeks out more and more.

So, you tell me, how important is it for you to use your voice wisely? Finding one's voice does not give you permission to hurt someone with your judgment. Use it from a place of confident certainty with a splash of empathy. Push back a troublesome client, fire your client (it's liberating), stop controlling an abusive behavior. I'm one for simply saying, "Knock it off," and that gets my point across. I have had plenty of years where my voice was inconsistent or compliant. No more. Men like to joke, and I have heard it before, that it must be menopause. No, I'm just dog-tired of putting up with your crap. As women age, we are much more mindful of our energy capacity and we carefully pick where we will put our attention. You don't get to take up my space anymore if you are clueless. Life is way too precious to be wasted on jerks or obligations that bring stressful feelings. There are obligations that must be tended to, but now I am much more mindful of choosing what brings value and joy to my life. You have one voice and sometimes you may only have one chance to make a significant difference in your life, so pick your words wisely and let your voice be heard.

SHAKE IT OFF: *What conversations in your professional and personal life do you need to have but are avoiding? If you used your voice wisely to make a change in your business or personal life, what would your life look like? Once I took the leap to have a difficult conversation, the quality of my life grew leaps and bounds. And yours will, too!!*

Life After 50—Achieving Joy Through Wisdom

There is no royal flower-strewn across the road
to success and if there is, I have not found it,
for what success I have obtained is the result
of many sleepless nights and real hard work

—Madam C.J. Walker

Turning 50 was the beginning of the best time in my life. My voice was starting to emerge with power and certainty like I had never experienced in my past. I could no longer hold back tolerations that seemed to take my life in a heavy direction. I had a family member ask me if I was still in menopause (a fact of life turned into an insulting label) after I stood up for myself. And, guys, this is a demeaning comment. Cut it out!! C'mon, why do women have to have a health reason to speak our minds rather than saying, "I just am not taking your shit anymore, how's them apples?" There is nothing more freeing than speaking what I feel when someone has crossed a line. And Beulah would declare repeatedly, "I am speaking my truth," yet my experience of her was she was so "untruthful," especially when it served her ego.

Enough of her. Let's get back to wisdom. It's like turning on the stove and, after getting burned once or even multiple times, I surrendered to "that's not happening again." I was running out of Band-Aids for all the burns and, after I used up my last bandage,

I said no more!! I can remember that day so clearly about a week after my brother died. I was still 49 but by some universal force, the voice Tommy left on earth found its way to my soul and I became Betsy × 10. The first conversation was flat out telling "Beulah" that I was no longer carrying her because I was not going to be six feet under like my brother. That opened the floodgates to give myself permission to communicate what I need and since then, I have been riding the wave called joy!

Not every day is perfect and there are still times when I feel like I swallowed a few canaries, but no longer am I held hostage by my own fear of standing up to controlling people. I was born to a controlling mother, so I have had to spend therapy dollars to identify it and curb it in my own self. So, don't think that I am a victim here as I have certainly dished out plenty of my own bull-shit over the years.

Yet, there is something about my fifties that allows me to inter-rupt madness around me whoever that may come from, includ-ing myself. I have learned a few lessons repeatedly, and there is so much joyful life to be lived that the lessons are few and far between. I read plenty of books on how to clear the clutter in my physical space and it was time to clear the people-clutter. It sounds insensitive, yet it was a necessary process as I started to peel back the layers of my life that were keeping me from feeling more hap-piness. Something had to shift. Some of us are guided to take that inventory along the way, and it's not always easy. That's why we see people addicted to food, substances, sex, power ... you name it. It's easier to numb it out than look at the warehouse of our own inventory called life. People have been thrown in jail for falsify-ing documents, so why are we allowing ourselves to falsify the threads of our behaviors? We may all be sitting in jail if that were the case. When we ignore the pain, we create our own endless personal prison terms and make it routine to be held hostage by behaviors and people.

There is something about looking at life through wiser eyes; through eyes that have experienced the ups and downs of life. Whether you are female or male, we can create new paths at any time in life. My personal motto emerged after I cleaned out the gunky people in my life, "If you have a dream and it means that much to you, take it all the way!" It does not matter what your age is to make a dream come true, and your age does not matter when it comes to making passionate career changes.

Once I cleaned out the toxicity from my company, I created a new workplace, rebranded, and took my newfound wisdom on an exhilarating ride. There are several endeavors that could have my interest, but when I took the blinders off, I saw this amazing company that needed some tender loving care. In 2012, at 51, when I took back the helm with a clear view, I had less weight on my shoulders and a group of people who had similar values. We all wanted to feel valued and cared for as we pulled the company out of debt. And we did, successfully.

Now, at 59, I sometimes scratch my head through challenges and feel the exhaustion of my pace. Yet, the fearlessness in me continues to move forward. There have been a few challenges on my plate that most people would have walked away from, but resilience is a strength and, with an amazing team cheering me on, I press forward.

In 2009, I started the process to apply for a coveted federal government certification called the 8(a). It is awarded to individuals in diverse groups who clearly demonstrate social and economic discrimination. The process is cumbersome and lengthy, including a narrative outlining events going back as far as college through present day. The actual application encompasses approximately six-plus inches of paper carefully tabbed with much repetitive information. I submitted the application and waited. Letters of clarification would come along with the letter of denial along with a long list of items to resubmit if I wanted to continue the process.

I kept going, giving the government whatever, they needed over a six-month period. And then silence, crickets, nothing for another six months. No matter who I reached out to, the answer was the same: The application is in review. Being a keen observer, I was attending a vendor outreach session for a branch of the federal government and, in a casual conversation with the Director of the Small Business Office (OSDBU—Office of Small Disadvantaged Business Utilization) she had served in a leadership role in the SBA's (Small Business Administration) 8(a) program. I shared with her my challenge and what came back was the reassurance, "Let me see what I can do." And that she did. Within two weeks, a letter came with yet more clarification of items to resubmit. I at least had some movement and proceeded forward responding to the various requests in the letter.

No matter your age, if you are pursuing a new business or a new dream, when you show up and engage in conversation, you never know who you may meet. If I hadn't attended that event, I would not have found a new advocate for my 8(a) process. Make sure when you are conversing about challenges, present yourself as a tenacious warrior not a cowardly complainer. Save the complaints for your drive home in private.

After my last round of resubmissions, a letter came with a final denial, but this time if I wanted to proceed, the application would go through an appeals process. By this time, I was steeped in the recession angst and it came down to the question: Do I invest more time and resources to chase this certification when I needed to focus on keeping the company afloat in turbulent times? If you were already an established government contractor, your company was safe from failure since the feds were still hiring. But being a newbie to the government space, every step I took was an important strategic move. The female attorney now assigned to my application explained the process fully and remained neutral until I submitted a formal letter to close my application. Once it was official, she shared with me her thoughts on my application and suggestions to improve my response. I was eligible to submit a new application from one year of the date of the official denial letter. We talked about my narrative and, at that point, I shared that I was LGBTQ. I was taken aback by her response, "Why didn't you disclose that in your narrative?" My answer was that I was afraid that there would be a homophobic reviewer and I wouldn't have a chance in hell to win. "Well," she said, "have you won yet?" Touché!!! I heard her loud and clear. Writing about my LGBTQ label would have been so freeing to include in the narrative.

Five years earlier, when I was in a grueling master's program, I wanted to quit in the same way I wanted to quit this 8(a) process and, back then, my wife said, "You'll be two years older and you'll either have your master's or you won't. Time won't stop just because you want to give up." This time around, she said, "You can be pissed off and give up or you can wait a year, write a stronger narrative, and win. Dust yourself off and go win the damn thing." Great advice and it showed up again. My wife is the wisest person I know.

Fast forward to 2014 when I resubmitted my 8(a) application. After about six months into it, I was introduced to a consultant who specialized in submitting 8(a) applications. He guided me to stop the process, hire him to put the package together, and resubmit. I had put so much work into the second application and my ego was screaming, "No way am I going to give up!" The consultant asked me, "How much do you want to win?" I paused, told my ego to take a hike, slept on it, and the next morning I stopped the process.

In March of 2016, I submitted a new application, this time utilizing the expertise of an 8(a) consultant. In September of 2016, AdNet was awarded 8(a) certifications based on Gender and LGBT Discrimination. SUCCESS!!! I was working from home that Monday when the letter arrived via email. I read it over twice, jumped up from my desk with tears of joy running down my face, and could barely get the words out to my wife, "WE WON THE 8(a)!" Oh, how I cried as she held me with such a smile on her face. The icing on the cake is that I am the first person to win the certification based partly by LGBT status. Winning for gender discrimination is a big win for women, which we all need to keep forwarding. Not only did I win for AdNet, but I opened the door for the LGBTQ community. This is a legacy win!!! A dream to help open a door that will last beyond my life.

I could have given up pursuing the 8(a) certification multiple times, but I kept going. Ten years from the time I submitted my initial application, my company is winning new opportunities because I refused to give up. And I get to be a proud LGBT-owned 8(a) in 2021. I would never have spoken those words professionally in 2010. Hey, I may be ten years older, but I have the certification!! This is just more evidence of why if you have a dream and it means that much to you, use your strengths and leverage your labels to TAKE IT ALL THE WAY!!

My hope is that as we read my words together, something that desperately needs attention will beep inside, and you take a look. Consider the number of times in our personal and professional lives where we acted as "fixer uppers" at different stages. Let this time of your life be your restoration. And you can re-create your home life and your career any time you want. Just do it.

SHAKE IT OFF: *Let the impossible empower you to keep going. Ask questions and pay attention to the answers whether you like them or not. If you want something badly enough never, EVER give up making that dream come true.*

A Typical Day

Leadership is not a position or a title,
it is action and example.

—Cory Booker

There are so many books out there outlining high-performance production if you follow specific roadmaps in your day. At this point in my career, I have read so many different plans by women and men declaring that if you follow their way, you will find success. Yes, that can be the case, yet a typical day is different depending on how you are wired and your career demands. The practice that has always grounded me, regardless of what is on my path for the day, is my morning reflection time. I wake up 6:30ish in the winter and 5:30ish in the spring and summer, often without an alarm clock, which is a blessing. Does that label me a morning person? Trust me, if I could sleep later, I would, but it's my work schedule swirling in my head that often dictates what time I get up. My body just tells me it's time whether I have had a coveted eight hours of sleep or not. The bed still gets made before I do anything else. Thanks, Mom, for instilling that practice!!! When my feet touch the floor, I don't race into "doing" a task other than helping my wife tend to our doggie. Once Gracie has what she needs, I head to a favorite chair near the fireplace and sit with eyes closed and palms resting on my lap. Thanking God for another day is my first thought, even when I know I am heading into a stress-filled day. I'm happy to say that since sobriety, my warrior self is very strong, and with God as my guide, any challenge can be overcome.

I do my best to sit in silence for a few minutes before I start my prayer ritual. Even the best meditators are overcome with racing thoughts. Whatever is going through your mind, stay with your meditation and gently acknowledge your thoughts and ask the universe to help you clear your mind. Anything we want to get better at requires practice. Stay with the quiet and don't let the racing thoughts deter you from your quest for quiet. Eventually, you will learn how to move your thoughts to the side and experience a sense of empty space in your mind. Even if you experience it for a few seconds, it will increase the more you give yourself this time.

Depending on my schedule for the day, I like to do a two- to three-mile jog alone or a fast walk with my wife and pup. When we start off the day with a walk, we talk through whatever is on our minds. That has a way of clearing out the cobwebs so we both can be fully present for each other and at the office. When there is inclement weather, we do a 30-minute stretch routine or yoga. And there are spurts where I don't do a thing, which makes me feel sluggish. Eventually, I get back on track. I have a healthy breakfast, head upstairs, get ready for work. Leaving the house with a kiss and "I love you" and "come home to me safe, tonight" is mandatory. If I leave first, I toot the horn three times for I-Love-You as I pass the house.

Ideally, I like to have 30 minutes to check emails and return critical phone calls before I jump into the pace of my day. Having a team with high integrity and compassionate personalities really makes the work fulfilling. Hey, we all would like to be on vacation often but that's not the way of business. So, when you get to be with people who are prideful of what we do and are just plain fun to be around, the world of work is much more joyful. Our culture at AdNet requires being intentional to maintain a holistic work environment. We talk through challenges and strategies. When one person on the team is out of sync, we acknowledge it and work toward a solution. With a 30-year-old business, periodically, there have been employees who are high maintenance, one who requires a lot of handholding or creates drama. That drains a team fast when so much effort goes toward one person. One person's performance has a high impact in a small company. When we have a weak link, we feel it exponentially. Drama gets tiring. That type of energy in a workplace has to be transitioned out sooner than later. It wears greatly on an entire team.

My weeks generally have me on the road developing new business, nurturing existing clients, and out there talking to corporations about the Maryland LGBT Chamber of Commerce, of which I am a co-founder and was president from 2017 to 2018. Though I proudly wear my introvert label, I am not shy about talking about what brings me joy. Finding people employment, which is the core capability of AdNet, and being open and authentic about opening the doors of opportunity for the LGBTQ business community energize me every day. Though I do like being in the office, if I find myself behind my desk for too long, I get bored. Being out in the community getting to know the inner workings of a corporation or the government is exciting to me. Writing proposals and managing our contracts is an interesting puzzle that is screaming for a solution. My art is to create solutions with and for our clients both internal and external. Now, we don't want problems every day, but the joy is in creating processes that mitigate problems or help contractors give voice to what may be of concern.

At the core of what I do is a passionate devotion to healthy leadership, which I weave into almost everything I bring to my business transactions. For all of us, when we have worked our hardest only to come across individuals who you can't ever make happy is one of the unpleasantries of leadership. I have learned to let it roll off my back, as best as I can, and move forward. Yes, I occasionally have sleepless nights as I work through strategies.

But that goes with the job. The world of social media fosters cowards in that there are many places people can stand on the sidelines and vent feelings without taking action or even coming to the table for an honest conversation. Again, in today's world of technology and conversation-less interactions, we as leaders have to develop a new set of skills to navigate the cowardly sharks out there who lack accountability. I continue to be accountable when the opportunity requires me to look at an action either my company or I took that reaped a dissatisfied response. Doing the right thing doesn't always make everyone happy but, in the end, doing the right thing has the best long-term outcome, even when it stings in the moment.

Consistent exercise and yoga help me to cleanse my psyche of things that are bothering me as well as support me in identifying solutions for work. Think about it, with movement, we can flush out creativity and process thoughts that can stagnate in our mind. I am at my happiest when I have a good exercise practice. Over the past year, my schedule has been overextended, thus lessening my availability for my usual weekend "Rundays." I certainly feel the void, yet the good news is that I can restart my practice at any time.

My evening schedule varies depending on my work commitments. My wife and I reserve Thursdays for date night, so we can have quiet time to catch up and giggle about whatever goofiness has crossed our paths that day. Life gets way too busy and it takes mindful practice to make sure we give our marriage quality time. Relationships need attention and nurturing, so when you get to go through life with a loving spouse, end your day with an "I love you" and never go to sleep angry. Before I close my eyes each night, I thank God for the blessings of the day and recite the Serenity Prayer. It calms my soul every time.

January and February are sluggish months for me with the darkness and cold. With my birthday in December, the holiday season is a favorite time of the year and January/February is an extra let down. Light is my medicine when depression looms. I pump up the fish oil and put one foot in front of the other to get out the door to jog. Running in the cold is exhilarating for me and supports the increase of my energy level.

There was a weekend when I was working on this book and everything was slow moving. I surrendered and got into bed at 8:00 each night that weekend with the hopes of getting back my groove. When my eyelids twitch, that's the sign to honor my tiredness. We do our best to retreat to our mountain cabin in West Virginia to escape the noise. This particular holiday weekend, I was in great need to immerse myself in silence. Mid-afternoon, I sunk into a long hot bath, which helped relax my aches and tension. By Sunday, I felt recharged and was grateful for a three-day weekend to continue my quiet respite.

Returning home from the weekend, I felt rested and ready to jump back into my pace. When I come off a bout of depression, I am extra vigilant with prayer and exercise to help ease my body and soul into my normal routine. Honor your feelings and talk about it. I shared my challenge with a trusted peer only to hear that he, too, manages depression amid a successful career and personal life. As with grief, I value the small stretches of time when the universe makes me stop. I don't ignore it anymore because I move through it faster when I tend to my self-care.

SHAKE IT OFF: *Embrace your routine and shake it up with something new to enhance your typical workday. Just give it your best and be okay with whatever your best looks like that day.*

.

II. LEVERAGE AND LOVE YOUR DIVERSITY

Silent No More

I raise up my voice—not so I can shout,
but so that those without a voice can be
heard … we cannot succeed when half
of us are held back.

—Malala Yousafzai

Your voice is priceless and your most important asset. The words we say and how we say them can make all the difference on the rate of our success. The Beulahs (Beulahs are female and male—don't be fooled by the name) think their voice is more important and will attempt to overpower through their words to make sure that you and anyone else who disagrees is silenced.

There was a time that the idea of pushing back against conflict scared the crap out of me. It's not like I love negative conflict, yet, in the past, I would rather have swept it under the rug, denied it, or been numbed to it. Those choices seemed like the path of least resistance, yet, in the end, it was taking a toll on my soul and my body. There were times when I felt like I was carrying the world with piles of baggage to wade through, hoping I could get to the other side. And oh, how well I learned to mask my angst. My wife didn't even know the depths of some of my business challenges. I came from a family system that made everything look perfect to the outside. My mother was the master teacher and I was always her good student. So, my survival skills over the years were to push through and not let them see me sweat. Don't get me wrong, in leadership, there is a time and place and the act of bravely moving ahead in the face of fear or disappointment is how we guide our teams. When you are at the helm of your company, employees want to see a courageous leader. What I have learned is that, when I bravely lead and am vulnerable at the same time, my employees get to put voice to their own feelings. We give it voice, put our plan to work, and move on.

People out there who must stop and talk about every minute detail are not the ones I am talking about here. For decades, I had to be silent in business settings about being gay and, certainly as women, our thoughts were second to men's. Unfortunately, that is still prevalent in our society. Yet, after the 2016 presidential election and the Women's and #metoo Movements have empowered us to Step Up and Step Out as we tell bad people to STEP OFF!! Bullies can show up in both genders, so don't read any of this as though women have been dumbed down by men. In business, I have experienced that women are not always supportive of another successful woman.

In the 1990s, I belonged to a professional woman's group and was also president of its Maryland chapter, one of the youngest women to hold the position at that time. As an up-and-coming successful business owner in my early thirties, I was surprised how I was excluded from inner circles of this group. The fifty-something crowd at the time had monthly gatherings of past presidents, and not one time was I invited. There was hurtful gossip going around about my sexuality, which was clearly an issue for the conservative elders. During my term, we increased membership by 50%, yet I was labeled as the Gay President rather than as being an effective leader. Within five years of the end of my term, there were two lesbian presidents, so, lucky me got to get the backward-thinking group ready for powerful LGBTQ leadership. Thankfully, it is an inclusive organization today.

Women are stepping forward and talking about our journeys of harassment in many forms. The stories need to be told and we need to be heard. Fortunately, we are no longer waiting for permission or approval. We are baring our souls to release the secrets that we have been carrying for years. I have a great deal of faith that as all these scandals are coming to the surface, we are breaking glass ceilings. We all want the glass to come crashing down, and we almost were there in the 2016 election, but we have more work to do. And we won't stop until we are held with the same equity and respect.

Harassment comes in many forms and, as women, we are subjected to high levels of abuse way more than is reported and probably more than we think. We have been marginalized for years and pushed into the background by men who think they are superior. I am grateful that I have been championed by many men throughout my career. Men who valued my opinion, empowered me to reach beyond my comfort zone, and supported me as I tapped into my courageous self. I was and am respected. And I earned it. Believe me, from the very beginning of my career, I held my own with powerful men. I wanted the success they had, so I learned to emulate the parts of their style that resonated for me. Make no mistake, I didn't act like a man to be part of the ol' boys' network. I politely (yes, a label commonly associated with women) challenged what I knew was wrong. Probably because of my family upbringing, I didn't embarrass a man in public and I would raise the issue afterward. One time, I openly challenged the CEO of a company I worked for in my twenties after he made a sexually suggestive comment to me in a staff meeting. I told him he was old enough to be my father and to stop it. Well, while we both smiled at each other, I caught hell after the meeting. He did say I had guts and he respected my comment, but don't ever say that to him in staff meeting. If I had an issue with anything he said, speak to him privately. So, I did get my hand slapped but it created a long-standing mutually respected relationship for years after. So much so that when I started my company in 1990, he drove to

Maryland from New Jersey to convince me to come back to his company. That was the best compliment I could have ever received from him, though I wasn't swayed by the compliments.

My family system first exposed me to women being marginalized. While the women were strong and independent, my mother elevated my brothers. My mother never held me back from my dreams, but expectations along the way were different. Let me be clear that, though my mother was stern and narrowminded, she always supported my career dreams and was always in the front row cheering me on with prideful tears in her eyes. Oh, how that woman pissed me off, yet, in her way, showed me how to seize the brass ring. She let many of her dreams go, so perhaps she lived some of her dreams through me.

The boys were given cars when they turned 17, not me. They came home whatever time they wanted, not me. The nights I rolled in way past curfew, there she was waiting from me—damn, caught again!! Their opinions were asked for and heard, not mine. As I got older, the inequities were more evident, and I navigated through as best as I could with much discomfort. My sister and I were held to a different standard but, in the end, we both made choices to live our lives how we wanted, not how my mother wanted. Then came the times when I fought back and fought back hard. Sometimes it felt like a battle leaving my emotions feeling traumatized as I drove back to Maryland. But I was not letting up nor being pushed around or treated like a game piece on a chess board. And my family experiences are mild as compared to some, yet they left scars. Those experiences molded me to handle some of the challenges that came my way as a business owner. So, find ways to identify the strengths that come from your family of origin; don't let them hold you back and don't be a victim of them. Overcome the demons. If your childhood continues to haunt you, have the memories and work with a therapist or spiritual guide who can support you to put these experiences in a peaceful place. Use your voice as a healing tool. The silence will fester and eventually show up in harmful ways along your journey.

As I have matured, when a man tries to bully me or my employees when doing business, I pick up the phone and interrupt the behavior. In recruiting, I directly see how salary negotiations are different for women and some of my clients try to undercut women with compensation. As soon as I sniff that nonsense, I stop it immediately. If we don't speak up, how is the other person going to know their actions are unacceptable? There are far more LGBTQ and gender protections in workplaces now that allow us to speak up, yet, still many remain silent and often go back in the closet. If that is where you need to be, just be where you feel safe. Those of us who are out there speaking up will continue to do so until equality for diversity is 100%. That may take a long time, but remember the women who fought for our right to vote? They didn't think it was possible in 1920 with the ratification of the 19th Amendment for women's equal voting rights. And the thought that same sex marriage would be legalized was a dream for many of us. Today, we are legal in the United States. Another example how a dream imagined is a reality.

Women still have to fight harder than men in business and it's just not fair how we have to keep digging into our reserves to break down doors to get our fair share. Being a lesbian in a business world monopolized by men has caused me great pain. But I am a warrior and, though there are days that the fight makes me weary, I won't tolerate bullshit from a disrespectful person regardless of gender. I can devote plenty of pages to experiences with the Beulahs, who were emotionally abusive women who were jealous, narcissistic, and great finger-pointers at others versus paying attention to the ugliness in their own mirror. It is when I found my voice that my courage re-emerged and the Beulahs started dropping like flies. It's an interesting discovery when how you show up in the world starts to attract difficult people and situations. I always thank the universe for the amazing support system of people in my life who show up consistently through the good and bad times. They lovingly nudged me to take leaps in my growth and were at my side through some of the darkest times in my life. My wife is my biggest champion who bandages my wounds and sends me back out the door.

I often feel like my old self was exorcised from my body when my brother Tommy died in 2011. My voice found its way again after being silenced for a number of years. No more did I endlessly give to people who were taking. Who are the takers in your life? In an exchange with a person who was a dear friend at the time, I questioned her behavior and what she came back with was, "How would you know what it's like to be a parent?" even when she knew that I was a stepparent and grandparent in my wife's family. That is one of the most harmful things anyone can say to a stepparent. And that comment was such a punch to my gut. It was cruel. Prior to 2011, I would not have even challenged that person, and it was not a heated conversation; I just mirrored back to her advice that she was always quick to dispense. After my several attempts to mend the friendship, it was clear our time was done. I waved the olive branch one last time and walked away knowing I had given my best. And proud that I stood up for myself. My voice was busy at work that year, clearing out relationships that were no longer in sync and making room for people who I missed having spent so much time with takers.

You will rediscover your voice when you take the time to listen to the voice within. At some point in time, we had our voice and, over time, events may have made us quieter. At times we give up, thinking what we have to say won't matter. Leadership books will tell you that often the quietest voice on the team has the best solution. Any good leader will listen to the quiet team member, so all feedback is offered toward a solution. Whether you are an individual or leading a team, pay attention to the quiet voice on the team, including your own. Don't contribute to the assumption that those labeled as quiet can't lead the team to a successful outcome. The quiet voice is equally as important when you create the space to listen to their feedback. Don't get swayed by the bravado. You need a balance of substance and high energy to take an idea over the finish line. It's your job, as the leader, to call forth the voices of everyone on your team. The success of your organization is dependent on your ability to support your teams to speak up. The leader is not the only voice in the room. Empower the quiet employees to break their silence and contribute to the conversation. And sometimes that takes you, as the leader, to pause and ask probing questions to discover their nuggets of wisdom.

Our intuition when nurtured is our most powerful resource. Yet, many times, we hear it and ignore it. Why? Oh, I can answer that, we think that maybe this time that person will have really changed. Remember, the leopard does NOT change its spots and ain't nobody else going to change. It is YOU and ME who must change our responses to their behavior. That can show up with voice or walking away. Just do something different if the interaction is still causing you angst. This applies in business. If an employee is still not doing what they say, the only way they have the opportunity to change is if you give voice to the change that is needed. Employees deserve the chance to improve the same way I do. Most humans don't read minds, so don't set yourself, your loved one, or your employee up for failure. Also, watch the warning signs for when it's time to walk away.

SHAKE IT OFF: *Your voice is your ticket to freedom. The first word may be the hardest but once you get the taste of liberation, you'll never stay silent again. Yeah, it's hard at first, but I promise it gets easier with repetition.*

Where Do You Fit?

Diversity is the magic. It is the first manifestation, the first beginning of the differentiation of a thing and of simple identity. The greater the diversity, the greater the perfection.

—Thomas Berry

The prevalent conversation since the 2016 presidential election is putting diversity and equality at the forefront of our focus. Though what goes on in politics is a backward view of "all men are created equal" … oh, back up a minute. They are, that's the problem: The men who wrote the Constitution were privileged Caucasian men. Silly me for thinking anything could be different by that phrase. When women speak out, we are given a plethora of labels such as *angry lesbian* or *man-hater* or *women's libber* or *activist*. What is very true is that I am an activist and finally proud of it. My activism is focused on advocating for the rights of all people, especially diverse populations. And for people who feel they don't have a voice or need help in finding their voice. Hey, look at me—my true voice didn't find its way out until I was 49 and I have never looked back. Sometimes, we all need a little help to speak up and that's why I'm writing this book because somewhere in your past you are probably from a diverse group that has been marginalized at some point in your life and are just plain sick of it.

I was there, and it started in my own family. When I saw that my opinions weren't valued and that I was expected to live life according to my mother's rules, I accepted a promotion, packed the moving truck, moved to Baltimore, and never looked back. That was over 30 years ago, and I would do it all again and again. There are still many times, as I drive back to Maryland, I step on the gas with gusto to get to my sanity. All I can say is thank God for my wife who keeps me grounded.

Oh, yeah, back to where we fit. There is a beautiful resilience to being in a diverse group. It is my experience that we work harder to get ahead of the entitled population. My experience in the LGBTQ space is that we spread the wealth and open doors for each other. Face it, the closet door has been staring us in the face for decades, so when someone opens a door, we run like hell through it. And we stay there. I always say, you can open a door for me because I'm an LGBTQ woman (and you can substitute any diverse category) and it's up to me to stay inside the "open" door because my company provides outstanding service. Stop for a moment, why in the heck should any company keep you as a supplier if your product is average? Don't get your entitled face on, thinking that you should be let in the door first all the time. Show why you are the best, get clear on your brand, and market the crap out of it. No one is going to hand you a damn thing unless you show up and deliver on what you say you are going to do. There are plenty of people out there who say whatever you want to hear, yet what sets the best businesses and employees apart are the ones who do what they say.

Determine where you fit. Some categories on business applications are obvious and some are not. Check all the legal categories where you fit. There are plenty of instances where people falsify their categories. Case in point, I am on a certification committee for a women's business organization. My role is to visit woman-owned businesses that are seeking certification. I interview them and verify the validity of their majority ownership. There have been a few instances where I walked in, the wife is there sitting at a postage-size stamp desk while hubby sits in a huge office. No lie, I was shadowing a longtime volunteer to learn the site visits and, on my first experience, she wants to let them slide. "Are you kidding me," I said to her. "I won't certify and I don't care how many years the company was certified." She pushed it through anyway and I still challenged it with the director. I didn't care that I was new on the committee. Too bad!! You smell like a fraud; you don't get by me for certification. I had the certification committee override my "decertification" because "they have always been certified." That was a perfect example of accepting the status quo, which was not okay with me. What do I look like, an idiot??? My role is to stop the fraudulent practices and it's a damn shame when other women are pushing the applications through because they don't want to cause waves. Unacceptable!! Those are the unethical practices we are interrupting!! Let me be clear, this is a fabulous organization doing good for women business owners; those behaviors were stopped as more volunteers spoke up about applications being pushed through. And the organization put more rigorous processes in place to ensure a woman-owned business was a legitimately 51% owned and operated by a woman.

If you are thinking about branching out to start or grow a business, take advantage of every learning opportunity that is presented to you. There are many and the key is to SHOW UP!! You'll hear me use this phrase repeatedly. It's true. Do you think business is going to come to you just because you ask for it once? The key is to get your name out there, have people recognize you, shake hands, network, and ask questions. This is not pushy or aggressive behavior. It is what you do to grow a business. Your interest and the tons of available free workshops out there will get you to where you want to go. Just work it and work it HARD!! I will provide resources for you at the back of the book.

I successfully guided my company through four economic downturns. Business is not for the faint of heart; we must be fearless and often proud to wear our badge of courage every day. When, though it's rare, someone calls me a bitch, I now say, "Thank you!!" They have no clue what to do with that answer.

If you want to consistently grow your business, use your diversity as an asset to gain valuable certifications and partner with the large corporations that are in need of meeting small business diversity goals. If they don't have us on their teams, they won't win the contracts. They need our products and services, so learn how to leverage your diversity and interrupt discrimination of any kind on your journey. Growing your business as a subcontractor is the smartest way to get your foot in the door of a government agency or large corporation. Just make sure you do your due diligence before you enter into a financial relationship. More on that later.

Career changes and business ownership cause us to be willing to step so far outside our comfort zone to the point of tears as we feel such exhilarating freedom. It is a journey where we are forced to admit our flaws, stand up to unethical work practices, work until we literally fall into bed at night, and the list goes on and on. There are huge payoffs for the sacrifices that have brought me much joy. Being part of an employee's success, whether that is reaching their financial goals or witnessing them to find their voice, get married, or start a family, had brought me more pleasure than monetary gain. It's the personal wins of my past that helped me ride the rollercoaster during the lean business years.

You will find that there are so many possibilities available to you once you open yourself to taking the leap.

SHAKE IT OFF: *You are never too old to learn and to grow. Take the initiative to show up and make yourself known. Let go of the ageist labels that don't serve you and embrace the labels that will get you to where you want to go.*

Powering Through Gender Discrimination

A gender-equal society would be one
where the word "gender" does not exist:
where everyone can be themselves.

—Gloria Steinem

The female label is one of such pride for half of the population. We come in all shapes, sizes, and colors. We bring rich experiences framed in wisdom and courage. For God's sake, many bring into the world the miracle of life, yet we are still number two on the food chain. And when we add to that label being a lesbian, or any background other than Caucasian, we are pushed farther back down the food chain. Though the gap is narrowing, women still earn 77% of every dollar compared to men. Black women earn 65% of the dollar. These statistics are deeply unsettling and just plain wrong. If a woman holds the same job as a man, she deserves the same pay. I don't think I'll ever shake off the anger I feel about compensation inequity.

When our gender continues to let our voices be heard on this injustice and fight back against the barriers that foster inequality, we will win this fight. You can already see that the younger generation is not tolerating separation and segregation of any type. Our female and male youth are fighting back the political machines to keep them safer from gun violence in schools. I believe that they will be a major force to have women paid an amount equal to what men make. The days of brute strength jobs once held by men are becoming extinct. So, what will men make up to try to keep us down? It will disappear the more we speak out. Look at the power of the Women's March on January 21, 2017. In a short time, an amazing movement was created to speak out against the disgusting rhetoric fanned by the 2016 presidential campaign. Regardless of the accuracy or inaccuracy of news reports, women and the men who support what's right have stepped up to say "no more" to the regard and treatment of women in and outside the workplace.

In the 1960s and 1970s, the Women's Lib movement leaders such as Betty Friedan, Gloria Steinem, Shirley Chisholm, and Bella Abzug, brought women to the next level of independence. As a youngster during that time, I remember listening to the news intently as they spoke out. My heroes still are women who didn't fit the traditional molds. I was mesmerized by Amelia Earhart as a young girl and read book after book about her famous flights and noticed how Charles Lindbergh was elevated to a more prominent level of accomplishment over her fearlessness. I would ask my mother why Lindbergh was more famous when I thought Earhart had more courage. My mother actually felt the same way but said that was just the way it was. My mother wanted to be a journalist, but her parents pointed her toward business/secretarial school because she was more likely to get a good job by not competing with men as a journalist. So, Mom, I'm writing this book with you in mind!!!

The cosmic joke here is that my first head-on experience of being marginalized as a woman came within my own family at my mother's doing. My brothers were always held at a more prominent place. They were given more privileges, allowed to come and go as they pleased, and their opinion mattered more. As I have shared previously, my sister and I, though 14 years apart in age, were held to a different standard, living under our mother's microscope.

There was no turning the other cheek when it came to the girls' choices. There were rules and expectations, which were neatly packaged labels that I discovered as I came of age. During my teenage years, I saw my brothers undermine her and each other time and time again. I was told I couldn't play basketball or softball because it was a boy's sport, yet I could play tennis. Fortunately, I loved tennis and captained my high school team, but she was not keeping me from playing the other sports. She wouldn't pick me up from practice, so I walked home. Screw that. I bucked her rules and, in return, I pulled really good grades, so she couldn't stop me as I played basketball, softball, and ran cross country.

While this marginalization could have impacted me negatively, I chose to let it fuel my competitiveness to be better than male counterparts in business. In the early days of AdNet, when I was given opportunities to get into a large company, if I had to cut my profit considerably to get the best person in the door faster than the large staffing companies, that's what I did. The majority of the time, these clients gave me an unviable order to start but as we proved ourselves and jumped through hoops to please the client, one order turned to two, then five, and then the relationship grew to long-term business. Many of my initial clients are still with us today. I was willing to go above and beyond to show my value and it was always my team's strong work ethic that won the business.

When you run a small business, you have to go above and beyond to keep the business on a long-term basis. And that strategy is for any small business regardless of your diversity label. If you act like a victim, that's what you will attract. Act like a winner and more good will come your way. It really works like that and it's simple with a lot of elbow grease behind it.

In 2015, I made a conscious choice to focus on attracting clients who did more meaningful work and, in turn, the nature of the contracts proved more gratifying to the individuals we placed. Believe me, when you are aligned with the mission of your clients, working extra hard brings more fulfillment in the long run. Yes, there are still a few clients we have and had that pay the bills, and you need that in a small business, but if a client's actions are not consistent with our mission, eventually, the client is phased out. True story: We had a long-standing relationship with another firm on several government contracts. We served as their subcontractor. The relationship was always collaborative. About a year ago, there was a noticeable shift in the interactions. They "stole" one of our employees overtly and became a delinquent payer and downright deadbeat customer. After numerous failed attempts to negotiate fair and reasonable compromises, AdNet, as a company, decided to turn over our efforts to our attorney and slowly phase out the business relationship. The CEO of that organization manipulated our kindness to stall payments. My final straw was receiving a condescending email from him with dismissive language. For me, that was like waving a red cape in front of a bull. He messed with me for the final time. In the end, we took him to court, settled where we were paid back, and, by mid-June 2019, our contract obligation was complete, which was three months earlier than the actual completion of the contract. Our contractors organically rolled off the contract and we were free.

When payment terms are specifically written in the teaming agreement as well as Prompt Pay is written into the federal government payment terms, the subcontractor can report the delinquent payments to the federal agency you are serving. It was a bold step, but I blew the whistle and we were paid faster. We are also nurturing a relationship with the agency directly where AdNet can become a prime contractor. Let me be clear that I crafted a well-thought strategy before I took each step. You will miss out on opportunities if you are a bull in a china shop and make hasty moves. Your wisdom will reap rewards every time. Trust it and BE BOLD!!

I thank my mother for helping me develop my determination. Each time I took on the challenge of her high expectations as well as outsmarted her to get my desired outcome, I was learning negotiations and strategy. She would move the bar higher and I would get over it however I could. It wasn't an option for me to give up because I was not going to let my friends tease me about having to stay home. Those early experiences can't be taught in a book. It really comes down to how badly you want whatever goal you are shooting for and whether you're going to rise up as a woman in a man's business world. I get frustrated sometimes and can rattle off the four-letter words about the disparity, but I have learned that the best revenge is success. So, I keep my eye on the goal and give it 100%.

Even in the LGBTQ community, a Caucasian male gets in the door faster than the rest of us. People seem to have an easier time with a well-dressed gay man over a well-dressed, attractive, well educated, highly poised lesbian. It's just ridiculous how much harder women must work, even within our own secondary diverse group. But let me tell you, that still fuels me because this girl works her ass off to deliver high-quality results, and I won't be second to any man who can't deliver. If you put the challenge in front of me, I will take it and if you want to succeed in business as a woman, at every turn, you take the opportunity to demonstrate your value. Don't go into the business relationship with your hand out because we are women. You go into that sales meeting very clear on your value and tangible results for the client to see. Then you can slip it in that you are a certified LGBTQ and/or woman-owned small business. That is the last line you deliver. Show your value first!!

Don't expect a handout. Expect repeat business after you have delivered extraordinary results. If you wave a large male-owned business or a small male-owned business in front of me, that's my checker flag to WIN. As a small business owner, you have to stay inspired and motivated, especially for your staff. Even on the tough days, you bring that fire in your belly to every transaction. And if you are not at your best, figure it out or, if you can take a break to get your wind back, then do it. Shake It Off!! I'll give you strategies that work for me on how I stay on my game even when I'm struggling in later chapters. Women are still lagging behind men in business and we have to act like Olympians at every turn. And it doesn't necessarily end at 5:00 p.m. Many of us must put on another warrior hat to take care of our kids, aging parents, animals, and tend to our marriages because a couple also needs plenty of attention to grow, regardless of how many years you are together.

I notice discrimination at a much greater level at this point in my life. Hearing or seeing any diverse group being treated as "less than" infuriates me. I take a stand on the issue immediately and will not tolerate that behavior in my professional and personal life anymore. In the past, I would sweep discriminating comments under the rug and often be afraid of speaking out—*not anymore.* My thoughts are known. Saying nothing also sends a message of acceptance of an inappropriate comment. In the 1980s, Silence = Death was used in the gay community as it related to the AIDS epidemic. That saying still resonates for me today because allowing my spirit to be beaten down is a pathway to death. When I speak up, my soul is alive and I feel empowered.

I assumed as I matured that women defended women unconditionally as a way of valuing our gender. Along the way, most of the painful experiences I encountered were from other women. It's not a given that we should expect our own gender to go the distance on our behalf, so be prepared. In business, I often see women are jealous of others' success and will stand in the way to keep another from getting ahead. It's like the "crabs in the bucket" theory. When you watch crabs in a bucket, you'll see some try to crawl out to freedom, but the other crabs are pulling them down, back into the bucket. When I step back to review those events in my life that tore my heart out, jealousy was the theme. Beulah rode the coattails of my success to the point that her narcissism made her claw to the front at any cost.

Jealousy is a form of fear, so what are we so afraid of? Our egos begin to take over to make sure we are recognized for something or other. Nothing was ever handed to me in my family or in business. I learned at an early age that if I wanted something, I had to work for it. I was fascinated by people, male and female, who got A's when they didn't study or by friends who had lots of dates or had business flying through the door. I liked being around those people because, rather than being jealous, I would observe their behaviors to see why the grades, the guys, or the money came so easily.

Well, what I found was that it wasn't always easy, they only showed the end result. And there is nothing wrong with that. The way I found out was to ask questions. Later in life, as I reconnected with old friends, they shared how, when grades came easy, there were other things that came really hard. I was shocked when I would hear things they admired about me that they wished they had. It was all said with kindness but it's interesting how I thought that person had it all when they were thinking *I* had it all and, at the same time, we were each struggling over the thing we wish we had.

Pay attention to women around you who use language that indicates they are jealous of another woman's success or any woman who has what they want. Don't contribute to these toxic conversations because it puts energy out into the universe that does not empower our gender. If you want what someone else has, learn how they achieved the success and mirror the behaviors that you feel will support your growth. Don't cave into harmful gossip. It serves no one.

At this point in my life, I pass along what I know to help support women and anyone who is seeking insight. Imagine if we all put out into the universe what we know. I bet there would be more successful businesses than failures. We would have more wealth than poverty and I could go down the list of all the goodness that would come from sharing resources. In the end, those who hold back out of fear or jealousy lose. Their scarcity approach reaps less. When I give, what comes back fills my inner being with joy, which fuels me to keep growing and improving my leadership. We all win.

So why do we tolerate discrimination and why do we discriminate each other? I guess if I could solve that problem, we would have world peace. In my corner of the world, it is empowering to see other women prosper and help them navigate the business road map. It seems like a simple formula that when women-owned businesses have healthy revenues, we will begin to exceed male-owned businesses thus diminishing the conversation that men do better in business than women. Current statistics published by the National Association of Women Business Owners (NAWBO) show how only 4.2% of the 11.6 million firms owned by women have revenues above $1million per year.[1] Why is that statistic so low? In addition to having a small business, we are raising kids, caring for aging parents, and often catering to the needs of a spouse. The man typically works late to get his job done and it's acceptable that he misses dinner, but a woman has to have everything in place for when he gets home, only to head back to her home office after the kids are asleep.

When you look at the pace we keep as women while building careers, shame on our own gender for standing in our own way. We have some responsibility in how the narrative is written and it's up to us to change the conversation.

I am proud to say in the LGBTQ space women are so supportive and we push each other to the front of the line for business. Our male counterparts are equally cheering us on and helping us open doors. Perhaps we all get how the toll of discrimination can impede our business opportunities, so we work together to succeed. That's the way it should always be.

---

[1] https://www.nawbo.org/resources/women-business-owner-statistics

Interestingly enough, I was president of a women's business group. At that time, I was their first openly gay president. My priority was to give members my business. When my wife and I moved into our home in 2000, we needed the house painted. I called Violet because she was a woman business owner and asked her for an estimate. She came over with her male business partner. We received estimates from three different vendors and did not select Violet's company. I came to find out a few months later that Violet went back to other people, one being Joan, who was a past president, and told Joan and several other women gathered for cocktails that Susan and I were all over each other when she was here giving us the estimate and that she was embarrassed. That was a complete lie. Basically, this group of women kept me out of the inner circle and hurt my ability to get business from other members because—from what I was told—there was a lot of mudslinging behind my back about being a lesbian (there's that "L" label again). So be it, I resigned my board position, which was the first time I threw in the towel and gave up. I let my membership lapse and never went back.

I had the good fortune of having strong male businessmen as mentors. They let me observe business transactions as a young professional. I asked to stick my neck out on the line to test waters and I was always warned of the storms I would encounter, but I took the chances and often succeeded. And I kept trying until I won. I keep at it, often tweaking the approach to figure out how to get to the finish line. That allowed me to build credibility and respect from my male counterparts. I'm not afraid to tell a guy to knock it off, always doing it with a smile on my face. Hey, I grew up with three older brothers, so I knew how to play the game and fought back when I was being picked on.

I can look back in my career and am grateful for the amazing businesspeople, female and male, who took me under their wing and offered guidance. Today, I surround myself with people who are givers. The day of having takers in my life is over and that has given me more energy to go out there and be great. I'm not saying that from an egotistical place. We are ALL great and our journey is to discover and nurture our individual greatness. We all have it.

> **SHAKE IT OFF:** *Write down the labels that you associate yourself with as well as the characteristics that are GREAT about yourself. Who do you need to surround yourself with to grow that greatness? Have you ever felt jealous about another woman's good fortune? What were you thinking and how did you behave as a result of those feelings? If you were not nice, how can you be happy for her? Notice the positive shift in your energy.*

It's Not Fair

*Women will change the nature of power,
rather than power changing the nature
of women ...*

—Congresswoman Bella Abzug

I remember those words so clearly when my mother yelled at me to come in the house. I was about 10 years old and engaged in a game of Hide and Seek with my neighborhood friends. Some boy next door ratted out my hiding place, so I was tagged. The boys were doing that to all the girls playing but never to each other. Even at a young age, I called it out. And shouted, "That's not fair!" and told the kid that wasn't okay. I was standing in the alley between my house and the neighbor. I guess my mom heard the altercation and came out to the side porch and proceeded to tell me that I had to come inside. My mouth dropped, and I said, "NO!! He was the one cheating." Well, that didn't matter, I was making too much noise and had to come inside. All I kept saying as I was crying and reluctantly walking to the door was, "It's not fair that he cheated and gets to stay outside and I have to come in!!" In my mother's wisdom, her response was, "He's a boy and you are not supposed to argue." Had to shake that one off quick or I would have been grounded for the rest of the day.

So, you see, I learned early on to squelch it and acquiesce to a boy and one who cheated at the game, no less. Like hell. I did my best growing up to not question her, but when my mother wasn't looking, I broke any rule possible it if got in the way of me getting what I wanted. Just so you know, my version of "getting what I want" was not destructive or manipulative; it was simply getting to do the things my friends got to do. My mother was so strict, but don't tell a young kid or teenager that she can't be a on the pep squad, attend a high school dance, stay out past 9:00 p.m., or even go on a date, for that matter. My mother held on tight, so I would be her perfect daughter. That's what my mother strived for, the perfect family image. I felt like a prisoner at 95 Rector Street, so any chance I could to get out, I would. I wanted to have the cool mothers my friends had, the ones who let them go to the mall, go to the movies, and do anything else that normal teenagers did. It took until I was almost 16 to start getting those privileges. My friends loved my mother because she always made time for them, or at least the ones she liked. And then there were a few who she didn't approve of for whatever stupid reason.

It seemed my mother loved the friends I had in grammar school, as she knew their parents well. But in high school, if she didn't know their parents, they didn't have a reputation that she approved of in town, or they lived life any differently than her rigid Roman Catholic ways, I had to work harder to have those friends get in her good graces. Here it was again; it just wasn't fair. I watched my brothers have some friends with questionable behaviors. Oh sure, it's totally fine that their friends came over drunk. I could smell the booze, but she couldn't. Or they came from a family that was not on my mother's approved list. It was different for my brothers. I can still remember a few of the battles between my sister and my mother. Similar arguments occurred 15 years later between my mother and myself. The arguing was the same. My mother didn't approve.

When I started my professional career, I had a few experiences where men were elevated higher than women. In the world of executive search, it was typically a man's game with few women allowed into the elite group of high-rolling money makers. We women were typically put into temporary staffing placement. I didn't mind because I loved what I did and I was really good at it. It wasn't until a female branch manager told me that I could not work an executive search order from Citicorp—which was a client that I brought in—because I wasn't on the executive search side of the house. Well, I wasn't having it. She told me NO and I got up, closed her door, and asked for 24 hours to work it. I said, "It's not fair," and Ella agreed that it wasn't fair, but that's the way it was. And that wasn't enough for me. I responded that she was a branch manager and vice president and I would work hard to earn her job someday but, for now, I was NOT passing the order I brought in to one of the guys. She didn't agree but she gave me a chance. And I came through and made the placement. It was my first executive search placement and the guys high-fived me, being genuinely happy that the young kid closed a deal. I went for it and won and, under those terms, it was very much a fair playing field. But there were more times than I can count where I was told to stay on my side of the business and leave the search to the men. The best way that I could say screw you to the jerks who held me back was by starting my own company where there were no gender rules on production. And that's what I did in 1990.

On to being a small business owner. That was another story.

I opened AdNet in February of 1990 with personal savings, money from my retirement account, and credit cards. I approached five banks for a $25,000 business loan to help grow the business. Those banks were Signet Bank, where AdNet had the business checking account, Maryland National Bank, First Fidelity Bank, Bank of Maryland, and Old Court Savings & Loan. I completed the loan application, brought in personal tax returns and copies of my personal bank accounts and investments. The first bank I met with was Signet, which seemed most likely to give me the loan because I had an established relationship for both business and personal accounts. The female banker I typically worked with set up a meeting with me and the Commercial Loan Officer, who was a man.

He looked over the application and asked me a series of questions:

1. Are you married? *No.*
2. How old are you? *28*
3. Who will pay this loan if you default? *I would not default because I had five years in the industry and already had clients. I had good credit and my family would help me if absolutely needed.*
4. You're not from here. *No, I relocated from New Jersey in 1987 and now have established myself in Maryland with no intention of moving back to New Jersey.*
5. Who is Michael Smith? *That is my business partner.*
6. Why isn't he here? *I am the majority partner.*
7. You own the majority of the company? *Yes, sir, I do. (The banker laughed and went on to ask, "How did that happen?")*

I sat there embarrassed and wanted to leave, but I knew the decision of being granted the loan was in his hands. I won the staring match until he looked away first. He quickly reviewed what I had attached to the application and said I would have an answer in a few weeks.

That same day, I went to Maryland National Bank and First Fidelity Bank. Again, both commercial loan officers were men. They went through the same drill asking personal questions about marriage, ownership, and my business partner.

All five banks sent rejection letters. I called each banker to ask specifically the reason why I was rejected and if there was any additional information I could provide to demonstrate my business worthiness. The answers were the same. They were not willing to take a chance on a new business that was owned by someone as young as I was. In closing, each said, "If you are still in business, come back in three years." I hung up the phone and shouted, "ASSHOLE!!"

It's Not Fair slapped me in the face yet again, but I wasn't willing to cave in. I only fought back harder. Fast forward to 1997 and the sense of sweet revenge started to feel really fair!!

In February of 1997, AdNet/AccountNet, held a line of credit through a bank based in Maryland. We had been doing business with this bank and had what I felt was a solid relationship. We paid our loans on time and referred the bank new business whenever possible. At the time for renewal of the line of credit, I had a series of communications with a banker who we will call Mr. Jones. As we were up for renewal, I had received a letter from Mr. Jones claiming that we were in default with the terms of the line of credit and that the line was in jeopardy of not being renewed. Addressing each issue in his letter, I demonstrated where we were in full compliance. Whenever he chose to respond to my letters or voicemails, he either contacted my Certified Public Accountant (CPA), Steve, directly or left condescending voicemails after business hours when he knew I was not in my office. Jones had my cell phone number, yet never called that number after hours. I had repeated requests to have a direct conversation, which he ignored.

He gave my company unreasonable deadlines to submit financial statements to file this renewal. He would ask for a 24-hour response. When we submitted what he requested, there was another request. After he did this a third time, I asked him for a complete list of additional information he needed so we could compile it at one time. Each time I went to my CPA to pull reporting outside of the normal day-to-day, I was charged $150 per hour, which was a hefty expense in 1995. Jones said he had everything needed. A few days later, he did it again. It appeared that he was trying to sabotage my business by not meeting a deadline and would then push to not extend the renewal. Steve and I worked diligently to gather and submit the documentation to the banker—which we did, quickly, much to Jones's surprise.

Much to our credit and equal fatigue, each challenge Jones put up, we managed to successfully achieve. However, I drew the line when the tone of conversations became increasingly degrading. Imagine a professional banker, Jones, calling me an "idiot and stupid broad." With that, I contacted the Vice President of Commercial Loans (his boss) of the bank with my complaints. Within two days, Jones was taken off our account, my line of credit was renewed, and we were extended additional monies on the line of credit balance. Sweet revenge. I stood up to the bully and he got slapped down. I won!!

One of Jones's comments was that I should cut my salary to pay off the line of credit. In the mid-1990s, my male counterparts were earning $150K and above. At that time, I was taking a salary of $75K because I was a responsible businessperson. During that time, I lost sleep and was literally sick to my stomach over the level of verbal abuse from this unexpected source. What was worse was that the treatment appeared to come out of nowhere. In later reflection, I noticed the difference when I first came to this bank for a line of credit, my salary was very low. As the company grew, my salary increased. Another bank later told me that they would have given us an immediate line of credit plus term out our existing line of credit.

The requests for documentation to support our line exceeded what was in our contract and, with his threatening to pull our financing, I felt that I had no choice but to give him every document and report requested. My company did not have the resources to have my attorney intervene and filing a lawsuit would have delayed the renewal of my loan plus cause more undo stress. So, I endured with the hopes of bringing this to completion. Theresa Finn, who was VP of Commercial Lending with "C" Bank, which I moved

AdNet's business to after my experience with "T" Bank, told me that "T" Bank was notorious for making female entrepreneurs use their attorney because Mr. Jones was friends with the attorney and wanted him to get the business. The attorney, in turn, overcharged the women. When I went to "C" Bank in 2000, I was given a choice to use my attorney or be charged a nominal fee of $350, which was the same to every business owner. "T" Bank's attorney charged AdNet approximately $1,446.85 for the same execution of documents. These guys were dirtbags!!

In 2008, I had an opportunity to transition to a team of female bankers with a competing bank who saw the value in AdNet and my leadership. I was over the moon to have a team of women handle AdNet's finances. We had a great relationship and there were no issues with lending us money at the onset of the recession. The business plan was strong with a strategy on how to shift the business model to the federal government with contracts pending. I made an easy and stress-free transition. The relationship was a good one. AdNet had been awarded a two million dollar contract and I had extensive conversations with the banker to put in place an SBA guaranteed line of credit to support the contract. The bankers were ecstatic to quickly get that level of business from us. All was in place: I went home for Christmas break and returned with a firm date of February 1 to start the contract. When I called the banker in mid-January to confirm we were all set, she said because we were the subcontractor, they could not increase the line of credit. I blasted into the phone, "We went through all of this in December and now it's a no? Are you fucking kidding me? You are going to walk away from two million dollars of business because AdNet is the subcontractor to a well-established large company?" She apologized for the mistake. I was disgusted and, against my professional nature, saw red and slammed down the phone. I put my head on the desk and felt myself tear up. "Damn her," I thought. "No one is going to get in our way of moving forward with this contract. I had a backup strategy ready in the event there was a glitch, and this was clearly a huge glitch. Always have a Plan B. With two weeks to spare, I had secured a relationship with a funding company and negotiated a good rate. They not only handled the funding, but also took care of the back-office payroll process. The relationship has grown and they are still my financing vendor today.

In 2012, AdNet experienced our next burst of growth and, with me taking back 100% ownership of the company, I wanted to consolidate debt at a lower interest rate. That's a good business decision. The bank had moved around staff and I was now working with the less experienced banker instead of the woman who handled the two million dollar contract fiasco. I called the new banker and she didn't want to consolidate my debt. I had good financial statements and had paid down a lot of recession debt. She didn't want to give me more money. "No, we are not doing this dance again," I told her firmly. I would have expected the female banker to take better care of my account. But she was not a strategic thinker and acted as if she knew absolutely nothing about small businesses. I was done!! My team worked our butts off to survive and eventually thrive after a devastating recession and I was not going to work with a banker who was not willing to be a collaborator.

Within one month, I moved to another bank and worked with an awesome male banker. We consolidated the debt at a low interest rate and he gave me a sizable line of credit (LOC) just in case I needed anything else. We still have a good relationship. Funny thing is he went to work for the bank that stiffed me on the two million dollar LOC promise and he tries his darnedest to bring me back. I keep telling him, "Mac, I adore you, but your bank is a road I won't travel again."

Through my entire career, I see bankers move from bank to bank. There should be a way to have small business owners from their portfolios provide references on their service. I'm sure if the whole picture of their career was revealed, the bad bankers would not keep getting recycled like an old tin can.

There are times in business when it's just not stinking fair but it's what you do with the adversity that will determine the outcome. I'm sure if I were a white male in business my company would be larger because guys get in the door faster. I have accepted that, yet it does not deter me from being a good leader and providing outstanding service to clients. I work hard and will always work hard simply because that is how I am wired and I truly love what I do. Putting people to work and finding them meaningful careers is a joy and a privilege. So, while some of the inner workings of business may not be fair all the time, I stay focused on my craft and, as long as I am presenting my best self forward and receiving the benefit of those efforts, then the universe is treating me fairly. Let the bigger picture guide you and stand up for yourself when you experience unfair treatment. The only way we, as women or any diverse category, can change the game rules is to interrupt the discrimination. Show your grit, don't sweep it under the rug, and let your intuition guide you.

SHAKE IT OFF: *You have choices when negotiating financing with a bank. There are many banks out there offering incentives to get diverse businesses in their portfolio. Shop around until you get what you want for your company. Vet them the way they vet us. Bankers are not small business owners. Never give all your power over to one entity. It will save you a lot of stress. And if the banker is discriminating, blow the whistle. They don't want lawsuits.*

III. NURTURING HEALTHY BUSINESS AND LIFE RELATIONSHIPS

Love and Marriage and Everything Grand

*Love is patient, love is kind. It does not envy,
it does not boast, it is not proud. It does not
dishonor others; it is not self-seeking. It always
protects always trusts, always hopes, always,
perseveres. Love never fails …*

—1 Corinthians 13

What is life without love? I owe so much of the joy in my life to my soul mate and wife, Susan. She sees when I can't see, she dusts me off and sends me out the door when I have little left to give, and she is my lifeline. Susan tells me, "Shake it off and lean into it." As soon as I hear those words, I take a deep breath and charge forward. We have been together since 1998 and were legally married in 2013. The happiest day of my life was the day we spoke our vows in front of our families. It was a perfect September day on our fifteenth anniversary. A long white stretch limo pulled up to the house and a red carpet had been rolled out for us. I felt like a princess that day, wearing a lace gown, hair perfectly coiffed, and a twinkle in my eye. Here I was at 51, getting married for the first time and feeling like a teenager. In the moments we spoke our vows, I was so certain, peaceful, and proud of our marriage. We deserved this day and it was sweet from beginning to end … and our relationship is still sweet, even after 22 years.

We had already been through so much as a couple—both wonderful and tragic, with falling in love so many years ago to co-parenting when I had no clue where I fit with two young adults as her kids. I was used to being focused on my career and caring for my mom, who was in New Jersey. I was in search of love, sometimes finding it and sometimes actually getting close to the right one only to have it not be the best fit. Then, one day, a blind date changed my life. I was cautious, having recently had my heart broken but my close friends were nudging me along to give love another try. We had a wonderful courtship, both a bit guarded and both wanting to find the right love that fit our souls. Interestingly enough, prior to meeting, we shared that we had written a wish list of the qualities that we wanted in a significant other. The universe heard and delivered the ideal partner. Now, 22 years later, we get to look back on the life we have built, which takes work.

The work is not about sweat and toil but rather making time for nurturing our love. We both have things that pull us away in other directions and at times we tap the other on the shoulder to remind us that we need to leave everything and everyone else behind and put us as #1. Sometimes it has to be more than a tap; sometimes it takes a plea of, "I really need you; I really need your attention to know you are there." I can be at my desk and Susan calls for me and my response is typically, "I'll be there shortly." Well that "shortly" is often one to two hours later. When I am in my zone, I want to stay in that energy because that is when I am my most creative with strategy or writing a proposal. This happens often in relationships with careers, raising families, or caring for aging parents. Think back to when we were in the early parts of love relationships; everything else could wait when it came to making love and spending time together. Yet, when our relationships mature, intimate time waits for everything else. Really, there should be nothing more important than our spouses. Who gets us through the tough times? Our spouses. Who accepts us unconditionally? Our spouses. I could go on and on. This is why fulfilling relationships make time for each other to balance out the life's requirements. Every time Susan and I go out on a date or hang out with friends, we get into bed at night giggling about the fun we had, and that quality time sets the stage for a happy week until our next date.

My travel to New Jersey to tend to my mom has been, at times, very tough over the years. After my dad died, my mom and I were connected at the hip. With me being six, we went most everywhere together and that continued through most of my life. All my siblings took on a caretaker role over the years. Fortunately, Mom was healthy up until she was 91, when dementia took hold along with mobility challenges. She is now 96 and lives in a dementia care facility, which gives me freedom. She is very happy and well cared for and I don't need to get home as often as before. Finally, I have more quality time to focus on my own life!!

The constant travel to New Jersey without my wife and going into the dysfunctional energy alone has caused stress at different points over time. Over the past few years, I have taken a stand that my wife and kids are first and family of origin stuff waits. It's not fair to be the person who always has to travel up and down the highway, be separated from my spouse, and expected to move my life around to be convenient for everyone else. It is very easy now for me to say no unless it's to spend time with my mom.

My wife is my best friend, my everything. I treasure the laughter and tenderness of our time together. We never search for things to talk about. We make each other laugh to the point of peeing in our pants. It just comes naturally and having both been #5 in our family pecking order, we understand so much about family dynamics. We both had parents and grandparents who looked at the world like Archie Bunker and we are soooo grateful that those traits did not find their way to us.

Through the hardest times in my life, Susan made it all go away even if only for a few minutes. She has a way of smoothing out my rough edges when I have had one of those days where I say, "I'm done with this business crap," and fire myself!! Oh yes, it's a wonderful practice for me to fire myself, get rid of a perspective that doesn't work, get a good night's sleep, and come to work with a new outlook. Susan is the one who props me up when I need an extra push to get out the door. If it's a day where I am bringing my lunch, there is usually a love note or some special treat she sneaks into my bag. She just knows how to make all the icky stuff go away. Truly, with her by my side, I can get through anything because I know she carries me when I need it the most. And I'm not an easy person who allows herself to be carried. It takes a lot for me to get to that point where I am waving an SOS flag. I push through whatever comes my way and look for the silver lining in any dreadful situation. My DNA has me wired that way, yet it's been since I ejected the Beulahs from my life that I now will ask for help when I need it and will say no to things that just don't fill my soul anymore.

A few months after my brother Tommy died in early 2011, I was getting into bed and feelings came over me that the world was crashing in. It was my first anxiety attack EVER and I felt myself losing control of my emotions. Business was in the toilet, I was burning through cash, liquidating hard-earned investments to keep the company afloat, and feeling the depths of intense grief for my brother. Susan reached over, pulled me close and hugged me as I sobbed from a deep place. I felt myself falling apart and couldn't reason through or find any silver lining for the depths of despair in my soul. As I cried, Susan whispered to me to say the Serenity Prayer and she repeated it over and over until I started to say it with her over and over. In about 10 minutes the crying was less. I could breathe normally. I continued praying, "God, grant me the serenity to accept the things I cannot change, the courage to change the things I can, and the wisdom to know the difference." She kept holding me close, stroking my hair until she no longer heard me praying. I fell asleep. She saved me from falling into an abyss because that night, I felt hopeless there was no possibility, no interest in trying anymore. During that time, I felt so much regret that God took my brother when, during the height of the recession, I would ask God to take me in my sleep so I didn't have to endure my failure. In my mind, God took my brother instead of me. He made a mistake and I felt so much guilt. God took the best one in our family and I couldn't understand why He didn't take me who was asking for a way out.

Susan breathed life back into my soul, she gave me hope, and I was able to get out of bed the next morning, puffy eyed, but my soul felt cleansed of the intense guilt that, in some way, I caused Tommy's death. Susan hugged me tightly before I walked out the door to the office and said, "Whatever happens with AdNet, we are in this together and I will always carry you through. Just remember, we have each other, always." I was now armed with the serenity and strength to turn around the company. I separated from a toxic business partner who was holding AdNet back and started on the journey to success. All because my wise wife taught me the Serenity Prayer, one of my greatest tools of leadership.

Having a soul mate to walk through life with, dream with, cry with, throw up your hands with, and pee in your pants with makes living worthwhile. And Susan is all of that and more, for and with me. I know as people get older, it can be harder to meet people, yet my hope is that people give it a try. Lately, I have heard so many wonderful stories of people who have lost spouses, took some time to grieve, and put themselves out there again. Now, they are in love, creating new lives and adventures with a partner. Why not? We have more to lose hiding our hearts or getting absorbed in addictions to cover up the loneliness. Why not enjoy a date rather than having another piece of pie in front of the TV? Oh, and the piece of pie is best when served with the one you love!!

Animals are also a big part of love. The devotion and commitment we have with animals is also an important part of the joy factor. Our animals rely on us for their care and, in return, they give us unconditional love like no other mortal being. No matter what the day has dropped on us, when we walk through the door in the evening, our pets think we are the best thing that has ever touched their world. They give us pure joy; they ask for our attention and time. Yes, different from our humans. If you are ever at our house or most any home with animals, there are several one-sided conversations that go on. Though our little sweeties can't talk to us, they communicate with their actions and eyes. And often times, they quietly ask us to slow down and pay attention to them. I truly believe that when I needed self-care, my dog, Bleu, knew and followed me until I sat down and placed half of her 80-pound body across my lap so I couldn't move. We taught her to ring a bell hanging from the door when she wanted to go out. And you better believe that no matter the time of day or night, when that bell rang, we ran to her. It only took us two months after Bleu died to bring another baby in the house. Our girl, Gracie, fills the house with energy, love, and loads of kisses. Our hearts are full again.

The most important part is to be in a relationship with yourself first. When you feel whole and happy, it's more likely that you will attract a life partner and/or relationships that fill your soul with joy. It's the same with business. When your business is healthy with a staff that operates with integrity, life feels balanced. I, as the CEO, am more energized to take on the mundane tasks that go along with visionary work. There has to be a balance, so it all gets done. And having the Serenity Prayer available to me any time is my subtle reminder that when my soul is calm, I am better equipped to be my best for my wife, myself, my family, and employees.

And when significant love is in your life, it makes the tough days a little more tolerable. As I drive home from those days, I always look forward to Susan opening the door with a happy face to make the bad stuff melt away.

SHAKE IT OFF: *Love is a risk that often brings the greatest riches in life. Whoever or whatever practice brings joy and love to your life, nurture the relationship because on those tough days, it will be* love *that makes everything work out.*

Your Workplace

We are not a team because we work together.
We are a team because we respect, trust,
and care for each other ...

—Unknown

If you are a leader, you have a responsibility to grow and nurture a healthy workplace. I admit that my workplace was not always healthy, having employed a few bullies along the way. Today, I am a different person for many reasons that I share through this book. My team today is a group of people who respect and honor each other's work contributions and life's journey. Having successfully come through four economic downturns, I learned in the last downturn how to better use resources. I kept the workforce lean and outsourced various parts of the company. When a leader in a small business has less to "manage," we are at our most creative, putting forth a solid vision, being very clear on our mission, and designing solid strategies.

I have seen leaders and managers stray from what matters when they get greedy. The recruiting industry is driven by production and results. Compensation has a commission/bonus component, which is meant to motivate staff to deliver volume results. From early on in my career, I loved what I did and still love placing an individual in a role that helps to grow their career. While there were commissions, the process to receive the commission was fun for me. I didn't mind the extra hours and, because

I figured out how to be efficient in the industry, I averaged a 40- to 50-hour work week depending on the client's requests. It was when I became a business owner that the work weeks averaged more than 60. But that comes with the territory. Anything in a production-driven environment has seen people get grabby to close the deal and make the extra commissions. Over 30 years, I have told my teams that if you have to cross your fingers for a placement to work, then don't move it forward. I have seen over and over again that this practice ends in disaster. It's a simple model to follow, yet many places in life, when we do this, the end result stinks.

For those of us successful in my industry, we make it look easy. Believe me, it's not, but the craft of recruiting came naturally for me and I seemed to move through the ups and downs with resiliency and kept at it until I mastered my art. While my role should always be as a visionary, I really enjoy working with my team on their respective tasks. We all work really well together and when one of us messes up, we own it, including myself, shake it off, and get back on the saddle. That's what teamwork is all about. Cheering each other on to win is part of our culture. We get that when one person wins, we all win and there are certainly days when we hang our heads in frustration.

What I appreciate and love about the culture that various employees and I created along the way is that our common thread is the desire to have a toxic-free environment where we collaborate, design, and grow together. Even with our losses, we grow. Postmortem analysis of victories and losses take place to identify common themes that work and don't work. I put myself under a microscope to make sure that, as the leader, I am still operating as a peer to achieve our goals and holding my own feet to the fire.

Through our internal and external vetting process we often hear ugly experiences that seem to be commonplace in today's workforce. Still, we hear how employees are verbally abused causing their essence to feel battered in their workplaces. In over 30 years,

AdNet has gone through several transformations where high producers and experts have come into the company only to unleash their old behaviors as they became comfortable in our environment. Please know that this is only a handful of the numerous people who have worked with my company. Yet, those few left behind various levels of rubble to be cleaned up. Early on, I tolerated bad behaviors to push revenue and for that I am not proud. With time, I learned that happiness did not come with strong profits. I can clearly pinpoint those times when money was flowing, and I felt so empty. Once I removed the final toxic bully from the space post-recession, I declared to my soul and a long-time key employee that we were creating a new culture that she and I always said was possible.

Since that conversation, we have hired individuals who really understood that putting people first was our #1 priority. Giving our customers the best service starts with how we treat each other and regard ourselves. We strive for work-life balance when possible because the reality is that sometimes efforts go beyond 40 hours. As an owner, I work well beyond 40 hours when it's necessary and, when I see the same people working overtime, I make sure we talk about being efficient during the regular workday to minimize extra hours.

It's an owner's responsibility to pay close attention to our teams. We are a representation of the company and ourselves. I remember before I owned a company, I looked at my work as a reflection of myself, not the company. I knew at a young age that when I did well, the company did well and when the company did well, the team won. What I resented over the years was working with people who focused on what they got without taking care of each other. When I use the term *taking care of*, that is not enabling, it is establishing trust for each other's work and making sure that our respective efforts are acknowledged. Part of that is also talking about the stuff that falls apart. I prefer having a gentle and firm style in leadership. If someone is running their own agenda and giving me or the team a snow job, I eventually transition them out of the company. It's my job to pay attention to the signs and feedback from my staff to make those decisions.

As my leadership style continues to evolve, I don't have time to waste tolerating people's dysfunctions in my workplace. It's like a poison that permeates the system. When not caught quickly, the damage can sometimes be long lasting, taking a long time to repair. I had to clean up my own culture and take responsibility knowing that delaying change took twice as long as restoring the peace.

When there were issues with a previous key leader in the company, after I finally exited the person, which was long overdue, my employees were feeling the same angst about what was occurring but didn't want to speak out because they thought I was over the moon about the person. I didn't communicate the concerns to my employees because it was a leadership issue and in my mind, it was up to me to solve the problem. I did my best from behind the scenes to change the behavior. One day, I was on a conference call with Beulah, my office door was open, and I couldn't hide my reaction to the nonsense I was hearing on the other end of the phone. I was done. A short time later, a key employee, who I trust with my life, shared that she had felt the same way about Beulah and was so glad to hear that I did, too. Within a very short time, Beulah was transitioned out of the company. Since that day, I encourage my team to always come to me when there is a concern with another team member. The deal was, and is, if you have an issue, you have to come with a solution. The conversation is to be accountable and forward-moving versus complaining for the sake of complaining. Well-thought strategies have come from those conversations, which have resulted in long-term benefits for the employees and our organization.

I ask anyone who is a small business owner, a key employee, a manager, or an employee to take an honest look at your current organization and ask these questions. Write out your response on paper or a computer and please be honest with your answers. You'll get to the solution if you take the time to explore the situation deeper.

1. Is there a member of your existing team who wears the labels of bully, toxic, or manipulator who makes coming to work a challenge?
2. Is this issue causing you to lose sleep or impacting your personal life?
3. If you knew there would be no repercussions to you, how would you change the situation? (There are certain workplaces, where you have to navigate organization politics to make change, so this is not always an easy change. But if you had the power, what would you do?)
4. If that person no longer worked for the company, how would you feel? Why?
5. Is the issue bad enough for you to fire the person or look for another job for yourself?
6. Who do you trust in the organization to share your experience with the goal to find a solution? This is not "water cooler" complaining. This conversation occurs with the specific purpose of finding a solution.
7. If this were your company, how would you handle it?
8. If you were the employee within an organization, how would you handle it?
9. What is the worst that could happen if you fired this person?
10. That person is really nice but are they performing their job improperly after a great deal of ongoing training? Why are you keeping them on your team?

Once you answer these questions, go back and review your answers. Go back to each question and create a pro/con list for each response, again asking yourself the pro and con to your answer. After you are complete doing these steps with each answer, you will drill down to your solution. Solution-based strategies are a work of art that takes shape with each thought. The process does not come out of thin air. You must take the quiet time to ask the hard questions, answer honestly, and look for the themes right in front of your face. Pay attention to the signs. There is always a solution in leadership. Don't walk away until you have explored your options. You owe that to yourself and your workplace.

If you have enabled or created a negative situation in your company, own it and change it. You are not a victim and don't get manipulated by people who play victim. Make a smart choice for your company and your team. Take action and follow it through. There will be times when you hire an employee with the best of intentions. Listen to their references and don't make an emotional hire because you like someone. Though chemistry is critical, if you ignore reference information or things that have occurred in the job history, you could be making an expensive error. From personal experience, I had a new hire who the team adored. Two out of three references were outstanding, but the questionable reference was the most revealing and wouldn't you know it, the issues we had with the employee were the exact concerns raised by the past employer. We didn't give it much attention and, in the end, this employee could not perform the job and wore us out with repeated training and personal drama being brought into the workplace.

Teams include really nice people and there are times a "nice" person is not always the best fit for your workplace. I'm guilty of holding onto super-nice people way too long. After you finally transition the person out, what you are left with is a mess to clean up that is costly to the organization. Managing a high-maintenance employee is simply exhausting and disempowering to the entire team, not just the leader. An effective team is accurate, meets deadlines, and serves both the customer and each other. Nice is an important quality but when you are part of a team, you have a responsibility to do your job as well.

A workplace should be regarded as a sacred environment that grow us technically and spiritually. That's just my opinion. When a past employee reaches back to me, and there are many, who value what they learned and apply it to current roles, that makes my heart so happy and the sleepless nights worth it. Being in a leadership position comes with a "role model" label that is an honor to wear. I always take it seriously when an individual brings themselves into my workplace. There are certainly times I wish I did a better job, but I used those stumbles to create the AdNet of today, which practices our tagline "Advocates for Workplace Excellence and Equality," which was collaboratively birthed with members of AdNet's team and me.

SHAKE IT OFF: *Invite employees to approach you, as the leader, with culture challenges and observations. They are the eyes into your organization and often provide a clear and objective view. Their feedback is your most valuable asset and helps to keep your workplace healthy and thriving.*

Consultants

I will not let anyone walk through
my mind with their dirty feet.

—Mahatma Gandhi

A good consultant is a gift and a bad consultant is a curse. As a small business owner, it's up to you to call the shots. Beulah started as a consultant and a damn good one. She established a great deal of trust with the employees and we could see tangible positive results. It was a good match. Eventually, she became an employee who initially produced strong results and fostered collaboration with staff. I offered a staggered ownership interest in the company after several years. She attempted to convince me that we had a strong relationship and that our level of trust did not require the insensitivity of a legal-driven Buy/Sell Agreement. In theory, it sounded like a nice idea, but my intuition and wise business sense said that the years I had built the company needed to be protected. The legal agreements were put in place much to her chagrin. Years later, that "insensitive" agreement was my recourse to get her out. A few of the employees who were there under her leadership have come back to AdNet since her exit and the stories we all shared about what we each experienced were eyebrow raising. It was a hard lesson learned and one that guided me to keep hired consultants at a healthy distance from the company. When they start crossing boundaries and inserting their personal agenda is when you must transition them out. Fortunately, I have two cream of the crop consultants who have been strategic advisors for the company consistently for the past five years. Along the way, there have been a few who as individuals were caring people, yet didn't understand the boundary of a consultant.

One of my favorites was a retired military executive who just told it like it is with a smile on his face. He came into the organization at a time when I needed a strong presence to help me navigate the corporate supplier diversity channels. Jim was direct and gave it to us straight. It was a style we needed to have in the culture. I had just lost my second brother and was in the process of a total rebrand of the company since I exited my business partner. The organization needed a total face-lift to clean out the cobwebs of dysfunction that creeped in with Beulah. Now the space was clean, and I wanted to accelerate our growth and corporate image. I knew that a direct and strong consultant was needed. Jim supported my business development efforts and co-facilitated strategic planning meetings. He knew a lot of people and, at conferences, would walk me up to contacts he had for years to help me initiate conversations. His advice was clear, "Just show up and get in front of the heavy hitters in the industry." I stood behind him like a quarterback being guided down the field by an offensive lineman and we plowed through the crowd to get to the people I needed to see. Jim also put me in touch with the company that helped me rewrite my 8(a) application, which ultimately led me to an award. Our arrangement was part time over the course of a year. Once we accomplished what I needed, his contract with AdNet was complete. Jim was a super person and I have the highest regard for him.

I went through two short-term consultant stints with people who were not professional consultants but rather left or were asked to leave their previous full-time roles and were looking for full-time employment. AdNet was an interim stop. RED FLAG!!!! The reasons why they exited their last role eventually rears its ugly head in your space. I had known Charlotte for a bunch of years when she worked for one of my vendors. Super person and we had a good relationship in that capacity. When I agreed to bring her on as a short-term part-time consultant, we laid out the terms of service up front along with my expectations. We were effective as a team to nurture corporate relationships but after a few clients visits I told her the reason I hired her was so she would go on these appointments without me, so my time is spent elsewhere. "Okay, I understand," was the response. Charlotte was a darned good salesperson, no question, but she wanted a buddy to collaborate. That's fine but in a consultant capacity, when there are clear objectives, the consultant is expected to tackle the deliverables. Yes, there is collaboration but a CEO in a small business wears many hats and, when I found myself covering my sales meetings plus attending with her, that was defeating the whole purpose of paying a consulting fee for an expert. Several times, Charlotte expressed wanting to be an employee of AdNet. We have a good culture where people are respected and valued. Each time, the answer was the same, that I didn't have the budget for a full-time employee at her level. But she kept asking and my answer was consistently, no.

The catalyst to end the contract was when we were at a training where each company in attendance worked together to formulate specific growth strategies. I was very clear about the direction we were heading. Charlotte had her own direction and could not make room for my ideas. She even went as far as raising her hand to ask the facilitator what to do. His response was, "As the consultant, you need to follow the client's agenda while offering your insights. You can't follow your agenda unless the client agrees and, if your client is telling you what direction they want to explore, then that's where you go first." Not enough for her. She dug her heels in and would not move. I was furious to the point I had to step out of the training room to cool down. I came back and was clear, this is the direction we go and there was no negotiating at this point in time. After the event, we left. I called her a few hours later to calmly talk it through to resolve the issue and put the consulting arrangement back on track. No response until the next day with a long, inappropriate, and emotional email. It was clear that the consultant had crossed boundary lines. She had her own agenda and became very needy. Charlotte had a big heart and worked hard, but she brought too much personal stuff into the space and lost her objectivity. I ended the contract and my employees were relieved. I have learned that I measure the pulse of a consultant's effectiveness by feedback from my staff. If I would have done that years ago, I would have found out my employees thought Beulah was a bully, too. Your team is your most valuable asset; use their wisdom to help steer the ship.

As a small business owner, financial resources are precious and I wisely spend mine. So, when I set expectations with consultants, I have learned to be clear and check in. Otherwise, you will have a rogue consultant who changes the rules to suit their agenda. If an expert tells you at the beginning that they are a "road warrior" and used to driving long commutes and then when they start the consulting engagement they attend the weekly touchpoint meetings at the office the first week and then start attending every other week, then shift to the third week, that's your sign that their own agenda game is starting. When they brag that they are an expert at a task, yet can't even proofread important marketing pieces correctly and I end up finding the mistakes, it's time to go. Consultants work for the business, not the other way around. If you see a consultant making mistakes, have a conversation. We are all human and get overwhelmed but when the conversations become too often, it's time to make a change. I learned after Beulah that I worked my butt off to create a company that does good things for people and no one gets to take advantage of a caring culture. Compassion does not mean laissez-fare behavior or that goals are pushed to the wayside. It means that when everything in a business is going right or when we are off track, we are guided by the truth and that can simply mean working together to get on track or transitioning someone out. And there will be times that transitions don't feel good in the moment. Yet if you, as the leader, know in your gut that the consultant is pulling your leg, it's time to let them go. The short-term discomfort will provide for long-term positive results.

SHAKE IT OFF: *Pay attention to individuals who market themselves as "consultants" who left their previous full-time job and are now looking for a new full-time job. If your intuition tells you the consultant is pushing their own agenda (you'll feel the certainty in your gut), it's time to transition them out quickly. A true consultant supports your vision and collaborates with you to create new possibilities.*

The Fakers and The Takers

*No one can make you feel inferior
without your consent.*

—Eleanor Roosevelt

Somewhere along the way, we all have come across the bigger-than-life people who appear to have it all, know it all, and want it all. We know who they are and we can feel them a mile away, yet sometimes we still get sucked into the web. When I have allowed that to happen it's because I didn't trust my intuition. Ah, there it is again, the trusty old intuition, which works every single time. As I said, this is a priceless gift we were all given at birth, yet we don't always listen to it. I really think that intuition is God's way of talking to me. And when I don't listen … BAM! I get smacked in the face every time and sometimes it has taken me a little longer to feel the hit over the head.

I can go as far back as college to identify specific people who I knew deep down were not good for me to be around, but I saw how my group of friends seemed to like that person, so I would think, "What's wrong with me or am I jealous?" Something along those lines that I was flawed and lo and behold, over the years, I come to find out that my friends thought that person was wiggy, too. We just never talked about it.

Even when my close friends would have someone come into their lives who I felt was not a good person, I would have a visceral reaction and learned over the years to keep those reactions to myself. Inevitably that person was bad news. I would sometimes be overcome with such intense emotion that I could foresee my friend going down a rabbit hole with that person. Sometimes, it would cause a rift between me and my friend yet, more often than not, when I distanced myself, my friend would come back to share about a bad interaction they had with the person. It is a gift and a curse all at the same time to be perceptive.

Though I have good intuition and can read people really well, I had a few doozies myself that caused a delay in college graduation, sent me down the path of functional addiction, and almost closed down a successful business. We all have our crosses to bear and, while we offer advice and write self-help books, the billionaires, spiritual leaders, and everyday person have all experienced people who tested our resolve.

My most challenging Faker/Taker was Beulah; remember early on I said we all have our own Beulahs? This one was the grand booby prize who came into my life at a time when I was ready to do the deep dive into my soul. This person appeared larger than life to many of us who were smart and wise; she was a very confident, engaging, and caring person who we all greatly admired. Beulah's own journey was impressive. So, as young up-and-coming professionals, many of us looked to her as a role model. She was results-driven and knew how to tackle the seemingly impossible. Who wouldn't be drawn to that energy?

The knowledge I learned through some of the hard lessons was invaluable as my leadership took shape over the years. So, while there were lots of walls to get over, the trail of wisdom left from the aftermath has made this time of my life infinitely joyful. I learned that my initial vision for AdNet was that people who interacted with us would feel Loved and Cared For. That was not language that was talked about in 1990, yet I spoke those words even before I met Beulah.

It was interesting how, after being around a narcissist, you can stand back and see that no amount of acknowledgment can fill the silo-sized ego they carry. Believe me, it was tiring to go back to restate things to this person if I didn't convey a communication perfectly or make sure that various activities pushed this person to the forefront as I became smaller in the background. My personality was not one to be dumbed down and forced to accept whatever her flavor of the week was—at the expense of my integrity and employees. So, as time wore on, I knew that I had changed who I was to make a lot of space for this person. Doesn't this sound like many abusive relationships? There is typically one person who shrinks and loses sight of who they are. I could not believe that after having done so much inner work I would get myself into this type of quagmire. One of my best friends told me years later that, after I invited Beulah to do business with me, Beulah said these words, "Now I'm going to make my million." If I would have been told that years ago, I probably would have never brought her into my company at a significant level. Another lesson is how when we have important information that could help a close friend, let them know. It would have been up to me to determine the next step but at least I would have had more of the pieces to the puzzle that would have revealed more of her intentions.

The first few years of the business relationship were exhilarating and fun. Past employees shared with me over the years that Beulah was a bully and they figured that if I approved of the behavior, they should, too. Behind the scenes, I was aching inside that this individual who claimed to love people was disrespecting my employees and I didn't have the courage to exit her from the company. Each time I would be ready to kick her out, I would allow myself to be manipulated right back to the same old behavior. She complained that employees who were not meeting goals were thieves. I remember looking at her as though she was nuts.

These were really good people. Ultimately, she was the biggest thief of all. But I can tell you, in the end, the best revenge was the success of the company and list of awards the company received after she was gone.

I shared earlier that, after the sudden death of my brother Tom, I found a stronger voice. With much clarity, I was ready to cut the cord and send that ship sailing. We parted ways and, after one year of waiting for Beulah to take some responsibility for debt left behind, it was clear to me that one more time the promises to offer to pay back debt were not coming. When Beulah was owed money, she was in your face to get every penny due to her. But this time, there was always an excuse and eventually she was long gone. Until the letter from my attorney landed on her doorstep, then suddenly, she re-emerged wanting to negotiate. You really must be kidding me. You don't negotiate with a taker. Delete-Delete-Delete!! The game was over.

I was reluctant to make the final push because I trusted that she would make good on her promises. WRONG! She was a bully and I was so worn out from the recession and losing my brother that I didn't think I had the courage to take the bold step with an attorney in tow. But I did have more than enough courage to take back what I created and worked hard to build. She rode on my coattails for years and was no longer welcomed. This person was in the way of my serenity and my dreams. Beulah's time was done and I was being called forth to shake off my fear, grab onto my courage, and clean her toxic energy out of my company. I could illustrate my process like standing on the edge of a diving board getting the guts to jump off for the first time. I turned around a few times before I shut my eyes and took the leap off the edge. Once I made my first jump, each time was higher and joyful with NO fear. This time, once my attorney mailed the letter and Beulah's phone call came, my fear was gone. AdNet and my leadership were reborn.

With the guidance of the universe, close friends, and a damn good attorney, I severed the ties. It was an arduous and expensive process, yet my journey to freedom was priceless and nothing would get in the way of my peace. When I completed the final transaction in 2014, I felt the final clump of extra weight lifted. I was free. SHAKE IT OFF, BABY!! Even with losing two brothers to sudden death, the quality of my life had grown exponentially once I closed that business chapter. The lesson was that, in 2000, I knew that this business relationship was abusive and I had to get out. I didn't listen to my intuition and kept trying to make it better and allowed the beating down to silence my voice. And the numbing out was a roller coaster of sheer exhaustion. It took insurmountable personal loss to open my eyes to see that I had the power all along to transform my life and my company into magnificence.

The recession was truly a gift in that I took business dealings by the neck and thrust my company into the federal government, which was our life saver. No matter what negative feedback I was given by the Negative Nellies in my company, I moved us forward. Those Fearful Fannies (oh, I have tons of names!!) found their way out of the company. That is what true leadership is about—staying on course through hard times and standing strong in the storm when everyone else runs for cover.

Aside from my personal experiences, I have sat in plenty of training rooms to listen to self-proclaimed gurus speaking words of compassion as they pick people's pockets. If you are looking for an answer to your problems, start with yourself and don't let anyone take away who you are. Just sit in your chair and watch their actions. And take the good stuff and use it but what does not serve you or rattles your intuition, leave behind. You must listen to your intuition to know what goes against who you are. And don't confuse this with stepping outside of your comfort zone.

Business owners and leaders, like myself, often reach outside of our day-to-day for training to strengthen our leadership skills. We seek expert guidance to grow our organizations and put forth our trust in experts who will guide us to discovering more effective ways to get from Point A to Point B. Our vulnerability is often revealed as we shed old skin to take our leadership to a new level. At my most vulnerable moments, I have learned, the hard way, to remain connected to my intuition. A Faker will capitalize on a weakness to further their own interests. Maintain strong boundaries and pay attention to red flags. Trust yourself first.

Look at Tony Robbins. He is a rag to riches story and has amassed a great deal of wealth by showing people who to be in the world at their optimal level. He walks his talk. When you watch Oprah Winfrey, she makes a huge difference around the world and she acknowledges her shortfalls while taking steps to shift what matters to her. When Oprah speaks, people listen and follow. Within the world of empowerment there are plenty of wannabes who talk a good game but are not walking their talk. Consider those who preach about growing businesses yet live in a life of scarcity living from sale to the next sale. Pay attention to those who are convincing you about spiritual practices yet look terribly unhealthy. And there are those who start off their trainings with meditation yet, when challenged, will shut you down. I have witnessed all of this and more while watching people get hammered for observing what inherently does not feel right.

After a while, I would sit back, watch closely, listen intently, and, 10 years ago, followed my intuition and exited the world of the manipulative mentors. All you have to do is pay attention to the cues of the trainer's life. If you hear stories that make you quietly raise a red flag to yourself, I guarantee you that what you are sensing is completely accurate. This feeling is very different from judgment—it's a poke in your gut that tells you that something just isn't right!!! When you are in search of empowerment workshops, do your research. Go where other people have experienced tangible results. Be careful of the Fakers and the Takers.

I often am called upon for my expertise in business growth yet will only take on projects in areas that I am certain that I can deliver exceptional and sustainable results for my clients. I don't dabble for the sake of earning a fee. As I teach the employees in my company, first rule is, if you have to cross your fingers to make it work, walk away from that deal. It explodes every time and often causes more work to clean up. Even in the worst of economic times, I have fired clients when I saw inappropriate activities or when clients verbally abused my staff. No amount of money is worth seeing my team demeaned. As a seasoned executive, I easily put clients in their place when necessary. If you don't respect the craft of AdNet, you'll be sent packing. Just remember, it might seem hard in the moment, but when you wash your soul and your company clean of fakers and takers, you'll open the space for more high-quality clients to emerge.

> **SHAKE IT OFF:** *When you see your financial and emotional resources going out the door to someone or something that isn't providing healthy value to your organization as promised, transition them out of your organization sooner rather than later.*

Crisis Leadership

*When someone is cruel or acts like a bully, you
don't stoop to their level. No, our motto is, when
they go low, we go high.*

—Michelle Obama

In the Spring of 2020, we were faced with the COVID-19 pandemic. Our new normal includes government directives to stay at home unless you are an essential employee required to be on-site. We are handling critical living tasks like grocery shopping, drugstore visits, and family care dressed in masks and gloves. Who would have ever thought in our lifetime something that would paralyze the entire world would happen? But then again, why not? Generations before us have endured plagues and wars, so perhaps it is our time to write our stories and outcomes.

Humanity is seeking leadership that—through times of such despair—is inspiring even when the news is bleak. Unfortunately, through 2020, we were not seeing resilient and empowering leadership from our President. He will go down in history as being negligent and ineffective on navigating crisis. Most of his daily press conferences were riddled with his habit of taking everything personally and insulting anyone who questioned his commentary.

Part of effective leadership is about having a wide breadth of perspective requiring collaboration across areas of expertise that are needed to come to a resolution. Some leaders have the ability to make quick decisions successfully, others need to analyze information in great detail before they can come to a decision, while others become paralyzed and put their heads in the sand, hoping doing nothing means it will work itself out. Throughout my career, I have been all of this, yet the head-in-the-sand approach stopped after I took my company back as 100% owner. No need to learn that lesson again!!

Today's COVID-19 crisis is seeing most every business being impacted in some way as we hold our breath to keep ourselves and loved ones healthy. New protocols and directives came up really quickly, advising us to stay home and to wear protective masks and gloves. These are now our new accessories until we know for sure that the crisis has passed. Crisis leadership requires a leader to speak the facts and guide us toward the most prudent steps to get us through a crisis as unharmed as possible. We have to be certain and courageous even when the news is bleak. An infusion of strong leadership gives us hope to keep pressing forward.

I got to the point where listening to daily press conferences was depressing instead of providing concrete answers. Losing trust in leaders weakens an entity whether that is a country or company. Yet, it also calls us forth to fill the gaps that ineffective leaders can't fill. We have the choice to accept the status quo or seek more effective people who lead us through crisis. Since we can't leave the United States during this crisis, we rely on scientists and health experts to provide concrete plans and factual information. My hope is that the youth of our country get to see poor and inspiring leadership styles side by side to compare and choose who they want to model. My hope is they see that emotional and erratic behaviors in leaders slows down progress.

We want our leaders to speak the truth and we want leaders to give their employees the real story, so people have an opportunity to be part of a solution. From the first week of the Maryland directive, the AdNet team immediately went to remote status. Everyone quickly transitioned all our work to home offices.

Fortunately, the nature of our work in the staffing industry made it easy to pivot. Our top priority was and still is to ensure the mental and physical well-being of our contract employees.

Over the course of the stay-at-home directive, we encountered employees in great distress. They stopped communicating about their projects. These behaviors were out of character, and my team made the decision to mask up and drive to employees' homes, knock on their doors, and help pull them away from the fragile ledge. As 2020 went into 2021, more employees lost loved ones to COVID-19. Just when we thought we caught our breath, there was another call about death. Our employees were trying to make sense out of not being able to have normal funeral services, not being able to hold each other tightly through grief, and being sent deeper into the emotional isolation of grief. There is no case study to follow, no books written yet on leadership through endless loss in such a short period of time.

We used our instincts and tapped into our love for each other to keep strong. Each week, one of our team would experience something bringing us to tears. On our daily video check-ins, we hugged each other over the airwaves and wiped each other's tears. What kept us strong was how we faced it head on and did not hold onto our feelings.

Seeing a need for spreading more optimism in the AdNet community, I started to write a weekly blog called "Tidbits of Joy," which contained inspirational quotes, empowering words from my heart, and websites of interest. After my workday was done on Monday evenings, I ate dinner and came back into my office to write whatever my intuition guided me to put into words. Go to AdNet's website www.adnetp3.com to read all the Tidbits, which will continue well beyond the COVID-19 crisis. I found that the weekly routine has given employees and clients a space to write back to share their own experiences. And it helps heal my soul from any topic that feels heavy.

A call came from my brother, Dave, the Tuesday after Easter saying my mom had showed minor symptoms of COVID while in her New Jersey long-term care facility. The doctor tested her and we eagerly waited for the results. Dave called me on Thursday morning to say Mom tested positive and she would be moved to isolation. I cried and could feel fear take over my body, knowing there was absolutely nothing I could do. I couldn't even be with her. That was the hardest for me to bear, knowing she had to go through this without the support of her family at her side. Surrender was the best I could talk myself into. And so, the journey began as we checked in daily for the status and called her, listening intently for a cough or anything that gave us an indication of her health.

She was angry the first night, having been moved to a new room with very few personal things. The worst thing to do for a dementia patient is to take them out of familiar surroundings. Her voice was agitated and she was quiet, not understanding why she had to be moved. Rather than tell her that she was COVID positive, I kept telling her that this was to protect her from the virus and that, at 95, she was in a very high-risk group. No matter how I tried to soothe her, I could feel her anger over the phone. I let her be and, when I called the next afternoon, she was fine. She understood why she was moved and actually liked her new single room. Mom's favorite nurse, Eva, was her primary caretaker and that made Mom really happy. Okay, I thought, this is good and we just have to remain stable for two weeks.

About a week later, Mom didn't want to get out of bed or eat. Not a good sign. She was put on IV fluids to prevent dehydration, which was the precautionary protocol for the residents. I prayed and prayed and prayed. Regardless of what I was going through, I had employees who lost loved ones and I turned my fear into focused compassion for them. I told myself that Mom lived a good life and, if this was the end, I asked God to make it peaceful and pain free. Then I surrendered and kept focusing outward. That helped me stay centered and hopeful. The next day, Mom emerged vibrant and ready to get out of bed. She got dressed and resumed her routine of reading the newspaper and listening to the news. The fluids energized her!! We breathed a sigh of relief. The next week, she remained consistently strong, as though nothing changed. At her full two-week mark, the doctor retested Mom and her results were negative. They moved her out of isolation and back to her room. Mom didn't remember any part of the two weeks in isolation and was beyond happy. I called her Miracle Mommy and told her that she should be proud that at 95 she recovered from this horrible virus. When I told her there was an article about a 104-year-old Italian woman who survived COVID, Mom wanted to know if she would make the news by surviving? I laughed. "No, Mom, we'll save the news story for when you turn 100," I told her. "Okay, I like that!!" was her reply. She dodged yet another bullet in her life and, with much relief, I slept like a baby that night.

The next day, which was a quiet Sunday, I was cleaning out a drawer when my phone rang from a business colleague worried about a distressed conversation he had with a mutual friend. I sprinted into my home office to find our friend's home address and called, only to have the same cause for concern. When I asked him, "Are you thinking about hurting yourself?" he started to cry and didn't answer and quickly ended the call. Among three of us, we were clear that an intervention was mandatory for his protection. Through phone calls, texts, and social media, we were able to find our friend and two of us went to his home. He wasn't there, so we asked the police to do a wellness check. It took a village to intervene. The pressures of his work and multiple family loss were more than he could handle that day.

Even very resilient people have been tested through COVID. Anytime you hear distress, take it seriously. If you put off checking in with the person until tomorrow—for someone who is suicidal—there may not be a tomorrow. Pay attention to conversations and trust your intuition.

I noticed my mood changed even hours after I came home from the visit with my friend. I became withdrawn and sad, only wanting to sit with my headphones on, listening to calming music. My wife stayed close. The immediate adrenaline rush rattled my core and a numbness came over my body for the rest of the night. Attempts at reading to take my mind off it were useless. The best remedy was to go to bed early and pray. Sleep was not so easy that night as I lay there praying our friend would find peace in his soul. As soon as Monday morning came, I sent him a text and he responded. I sent him the Serenity Prayer that got me through my own dark moments. The day went on and, knowing he was okay and knowing Mom was okay, I got through my day.

As I write this chapter, the path to resuming life as we all know it is still very uncertain. We are still home and will remain here until we feel comfortable to go into crowds. For those who are protesting and arguing that their freedoms are being violated, just shut up and stay the hell home. Focus on supporting small businesses and creating a village of resources for those who have lost jobs and closed their businesses. When we work together, we will get through the worst of times. Fighting will not get us past COVID any faster. With a sense of calm in one's soul, we can find the resolve we need to get to the next day.

Amid COVID-19 came the killing of George Floyd and the escalated lack of tolerance for police brutality toward the black community. Racism is poison and evil that continues to run through the veins of bad people. My heart aches and all I want is to be part of the solution to end this gross behavior. Sadly, through social media and general conversations, I am seeing how racism is prevalent in the minds of people I respect and love. My opinion of them has changed and, rather than jumping onto the hate bus, I am asking questions, eloquently challenging their views, and educating by sending neutral articles and data with the hopes I can open one mind and heart at a time.

My company was founded on the expectation that anyone who interacts with us walks away feeling loved. It was an unusual and perhaps naive view 30 years ago, but I stand by that vision today. There have certainly been people who we can't make happy for whatever reason, but we make sure everyone feels heard so we can come to a compromise as best as we can.

AdNet will never allow social injustice of any kind to any person, for any reason. I won't speak for my employees, but I am 100% in support of the Black Lives Matter movement because I truly believe that when we end harm to the black community, the other equality movements will be honored. We have to make the world safe for everyone and it is our duty as leaders to start within our organizations to set this culture and stop racist behavior. When we start to show others the way a white person grips tightly to their privilege, it breeds hate. We can use privilege to end racism. And, as a white person, using my influence to interrupt narrow-minded opinions and hateful behavior adds to a solution. Imagine if every leader did their part to make social justice the norm. We would get close to peace much quicker. In my mind, that responsibility is a must.

As leaders, to lead the charge of well-being and positive change, we must take care of ourselves, so we think clearly in order to lead our organizations and communities. The most overused word right now is "pivot," which is necessary to recover the business we lost or at least shift our state of mind to adjust to what is and rebuild for the future. If you have resilience, you will get to the other side. If you don't feel resilient, dig deep and reach out for support. We don't have to tackle this deadly time alone. Talk about it, cry about it, scream about it. And, once you release the feelings, regroup and create your plan to move forward.

My silver lining through this time was to have the slower pace to admit that the way my schedule is set up is not how I want to operate going forward. Frenetically being on the road from one end of the region to the other is wearing me out. I love my work and it is my craft. So, why was I fatigued and why do I come home at night rung out? Early on into the pandemic, I changed my diet and took off a little weight. That motivated me to start working out again. The arthritis in my legs went away, I was sleeping better, and my energy was really good.

This told me that when our state returns to our new norm of business, I will return a changed person. I figured out how to reorganize my schedule to travel more effectively and I finally hired an assistant to support my sales efforts so I can focus on the areas of the business that I love while she handles the research and translates my ideas into impactful outreach.

As far as my employees, no one returns to the office unless they feel safe. Through crises we have seen that we carried each other no matter what we felt or what we looked like over video conference. What has been consistent is our desire for a peaceful world filled with heart-driven possibility.

Our allegiance is to each other and our purpose.

SHAKE IT OFF: *In the face of crisis, the only choice is to work together and listen intently to each other. Crisis and unrest present us with opportunities to change our future and give leaders at all levels a front seat to creating an equitable world.*

IV. HEALTH

Burnout

For fast soothing relief, try slowing down …

—Lily Tomlin

Sometimes burnout is the elephant in the room that we don't want to admit we are experiencing. It is an admission that we are tired and, frankly, hit a wall with little ability to bounce back quickly. The rubber band won't give and the cement feels thicker and thicker. I'm actually in the middle of it as I write because it seemed like the perfect time to describe the feelings. What I know is that burnout is a normal experience for anyone in business. The overload of technology today adds to our requirement to absorb tons of information whether or not we want it. Everywhere we turn, there is information. It's too much and sometimes our bodies have had enough of our abuse. We scream for rest. So, cut it out, stop, and listen. Here is what it sounds like …

There is a feeling of intense exhaustion as I push myself through being on automatic. I have to operate from that place because business does not stop because I have nothing more to give. I tend to move things around my desk, get small tasks done because my attention span is very frenetic. Don't even try to pick up the phone to do sales calls because the thought of having to pump out numbers is more than I can even fathom. The worst part is when I have had to push through like recently, I was in the process of writing an important proposal response, so the deadline was not going to wait for me to get my groove back. It started to show up on a Wednesday and I could feel myself losing steam and feeling very distracted. It took me forever to get started writing, so what worked is that I wrote the easy parts that didn't require creativity. At least I could check off my to-do list. By Friday I gave myself a deadline, which I accomplished. Then I would be done for the weekend but nope, not me, I kept on going. We headed to the mountains in West Virginia, where I could quiet the noise in my head. It was easy for me to spend time working on this book because it was a joyful process where I could mind dump and cleanse my soul. The weekend went by fast and it was already Monday, which is a remote day for me, and I was so grateful to be able to stay home.

Burnout pushes me into solitude where I can begin to find my center again. Yet, meditating is scattered and my mind swirls non-stop. That Monday came and all I could do was put on my sneakers and go for a brisk walk with my wife. It was another cold and gray day out, which does not help. It feels like the type of day where I want to stay in bed and pull the covers over my head. I can count on both hands the number of times I allowed myself that delicious luxury throughout my life. My DNA just doesn't allow for staying in bed. It has me feel like I am letting my circumstances control me and my personality doesn't allow for me to give up but rather to find another way. I fight back. That sounds like a badge of honor and not one to be proud of. Once I turned 50, I learned to lean into burnout because it is a wise process for well-being. I may not like it, yet I have accepted, finally, that I am not superwoman and don't want to be anymore.

I pushed myself to work on the proposal and went right to the intense sections to get the hard stuff done. Once I had the framework in place, I could get a good night sleep and review it on Tuesday with fresh eyes. As 5:30 p.m. approached, my eyes were burning and there was nothing more to give. I think I pushed it too far because that feeling of intense exhaustion had returned. This crap started five days ago, and I was feeling worse. How in the hell was I going to show up at the office on Tuesday to lead the charge and infuse more energy into an already animated team? Crap, just go to bed and it will be all better in the morning. WRONG!! When I am in proposal mode, I create in my dreams and think of where to tweak my writing. So, then I lay there awake and get myself back to sleep by imagining myself at the beach with sun on my face. Finally, I fall back to sleep.

Tuesday morning came and when I opened my eyes it was clear that the exhaustion was still there. Damn it!! How do I get my groove back? Stay home and get over yourself that you need a mental health day! There is no such thing as mental health rest day with a blasted proposal due. It was a warm day, so I put on my sneakers and walked again. That helped. Came home, took a hot shower, and dressed. What was my plan for the day? Go meditate, pray, and get to my desk. That helped, and I took one line at a time. We had started setting our deadlines to submit proposals two days beforehand, so I still had about a week before the due date. So glad I changed our mindset to get proposals done a few days early. This extra time really helped me get through this temporary blip in my energy.

I headed up to bed at 8:30 that evening. What has always worked for me is to go to bed early on days when I'm feeling the pangs of burnout and allow myself to wake up naturally the next morning. My body clock has changed in my fifties, where I naturally wake up early no matter what time I get to sleep. Occasionally I'll sleep past 8:00 but that only seems to be while I'm on vacation. Somehow, I just know that there is way too much to get accomplished before my energy gets away from me by the end of the day.

I wanted to finish up a book but as I turned the page to one of the last chapters, I was ready for sleep. Rather than push myself to get to the end, something had me quickly close the book and turn out the light. My evening practice is to say the Serenity Prayer, thank God for life and do the 4-7-8 Breath practice (there are many variations), which helps to calm myself and fall asleep (sometimes!!). I take in a hearty breath for 4 seconds, hold it for 7 seconds, and exhale for 8 seconds. I do that four times and then hope to fall asleep. It worked and I was out cold. I didn't even hear my wife come to bed.

When I woke up a little after 6:00 the next morning, I was actually afraid that the burnout demon might still be lurking. As usual, I said to myself that enough is enough and allowed myself to gently emerge. One foot went in front of the other and, eventually, I was downstairs feeling like myself again. This time, I headed for my meditation spot first, after feeding our animals. They always come first, no matter how we feel. Meditation is my life saver. It doesn't have to look a certain way. Just find a quiet spot, sit still, and empty your mind as best as you can. It's been about 15 years since I started a meditation practice and some days my mind is empty and some days I can't focus at all, but the end result still leaves me calmer than when I started. So, don't give up even if five minutes of stillness feels like an eternity. Consider it a gift that helps you balance work and home.

Think about all the time we devote to our work, thinking and overthinking every task that is presented as a business owner and leader. Yet, we find it so hard to put aside a small block of time for stillness. It took me a long time to discover the benefits but, when I did, it felt like a blessing. Part of my meditations are daily prayers, speaking gratitude in my life, and just simply having nothing in my mind. It's tough for a Type A overachiever to do that and with practice you will find peace. Some of my best business decisions come after my quiet time. There are also times that I speak out loud or write down the problem before I go to bed and ask God for clarity when I wake up. Never once have I been let down. The answer comes and I'm ready to face the day. God ALWAYS gives me what I need.

And, you bet when I am burnt out, I am praying hard to get my groove back. Having to surrender that I can't do one more stitch of work is difficult. I'm a small business owner with some hefty goals to accomplish over the next five years. It's an important time for me at this stage of my career. My company is positioned with coveted federal certifications and long-term contracts in place. In my mind, every moment counts. When I think that my two brothers died at 59 and 62, there is so much left for me to experience, yet the way to keep living a full life is to take care of myself first. So, I have learned that when the universe drops burnout on my plate, I am being messaged to slow the heck down and get some rest.

When I went back to the office on Wednesday, I felt loved and missed and jumped right back into the groove. Feeling cared for at work makes a huge difference for my energy and motivation. I would do anything for my staff, truly. They are my professional lifeline and I take it seriously that they choose to work at my company through the best and the worst of times. I'm so grateful.

My best advice for burnout is to start with easy remedies like leaving work a little early to go home and put your feet up. While one would say that exercise will make you feel better, putting yourself in continuous motion will not heal the burnout. You must STOP and rest. Go home, take a hot bath, make a cup of tea, find your favorite chair, and put your feet up. Avoid alcohol or any mind-altering substance. If you are going to indulge in something sweet, have a normal portion, don't overeat. You must nurture yourself back. And if you just want to sob, do it. Exhaustion pushes us to the edge and will evoke multiple emotions. Embrace and feel those emotions because bottling everything up will just eventually boil over and that will prolong the burnout.

Get into bed early and if you have to wake up naturally or move around your calendar the next day then do it. Wake up whenever you wake up, meditate or pray, and go for a walk. Just find a way to quiet your mind before you pick up your briefcase and head out the door. Once you get to the office, take about 30 minutes by yourself to check your email, get your day planned, and ease into your pace. Remember, burnout does not go away overnight so give yourself a day or two with an easy schedule if you can. If you have to keep up your daily schedule, do your best to leave the office at a reasonable time and keep your evening quiet. Small business owners can't just hop on a plane for a relaxing escape. We have to practice self-care in increments as we take care of business.

You can shake off the worst of burnout when you take care of yourself.

Recently, I had a minor health scare that shook me enough to pay attention. I'm healthy and active at 59, yet my family history forces me to be very mindful of my health. This incident rattled me enough to close down all technology when I went on vacation. My psyche needed a break. When I returned to work, I delegated more often, asked for what I needed, and took a step back from some of my community involvement. My priority was to get my health back on track. Let your well-being fuel you, not your ego. When you are at your best, everything around you feels so much more joyful.

SHAKE IT OFF: *If you don't stop your body, your body will stop you regardless of what you want. So, give yourself an extended short-term "time-out" for long-term health to shake off your exhaustion. The result will be a clear head and a re-energized leader. You and your workplace team deserve it.*

Unpick Your Poison

*Be good to the living because
when you're dead, you're dead.*

—John Cerulo, Sr. (my dad)

This was my father's mantra and he was so right. Who cares if you are crying over a loved one's coffin? Once we are dead, that's it. No rewind. No second chance. It's final, yet we think it can wait until tomorrow. I lost two siblings in an 18-month period—talk about taking one's breath away. Geez, I had just recovered and gotten myself and my company back on track when BAM, Jack died. Another heart attack and another brother died alone. This was just flipping crazy and I had no choice but to suck it up, deal with it, grieve it, and get on with life or sink in the quicksand of loss. I have a lot of life left ahead of me and I had to embrace my new normal to be able to find my footing.

How could God do this to me a second time? My brother Jack had come down to Maryland to see my new office a week before. The recession almost brought my company to its knees and, through it all, Jack said, "Stay with it because you will be stronger on the other side of it and you know what to do." Jack was my business confidante and I felt so proud that he wanted to come down to see my office. I had majorly downsized during the recession and now was upsizing, and Jack wanted to cheer me on. We had a great time seeing a Yankees game, eating hot dogs, and laughing about our family. We said goodbye as Jack and his wife drove off in their convertible headed to the beach. How would I know that was the last time I would ever see him again?

Susan and I had sold our condo in South Florida and were moving our stuff back to Maryland. We had just emptied the truck and I got a call from my nephew saying, "Aunt Betsy, my father died." Damn it, those words just ripped through me. This is a bad dream and can't be happening to me again. Not Jack!!! He had a great family, a new house at the Jersey shore, a condo on the beach, and was highly respected in the community. Another pillar gone, just gone!!! At least I got to have a wonderful visit and tell him I loved him a few days before he was taken.

That was enough for me, I was done with these losses, yet this time I felt like an old hand and walked through this loss feeling much stronger. I just put one foot in front of the other, took back out my grief meditation book, and resumed my grieving process. This time felt different, a little easier as I kept numbing myself. There was so much ahead for me to look forward to. Susan and I were getting married in a few months, AdNet had recovered from the recession, and we were getting stronger. Everything was looking good except I was living my own lie.

Be good to the living, my father would say, yet I'll never know if he was also talking about himself. He died at 49 in a car crash, a life cut short when there was so much life to live. I wanted to live. I wanted to live a long and healthy life like my grandmother and mother. Perhaps, I needed to start with myself before I became the next family statistic.

And it was Jack's death that had me take the most courageous step in my life. It was time to give up my biggest demon: alcohol. Losing two brothers to sudden heart attacks was a good time to take an inventory of my life. This was the final wakeup call that I needed, and I was ready. It was Friday the 13th when I said, NO MORE!! I had been wanting to stop for years. There was no exciting story to share, no blackouts for weeks, no lost job, no impact in finances. I was a functioning alcoholic, which is a tough label to admit—quietly drowning in my addiction except for a few friends who knew of my struggle. The next day, I found an Alcoholics Anonymous meeting and there it was on the table with a bunch of literature: A Spiritual Retreat for AA Members at Holy Trinity Monastery. HOLY CRAP!!! That was at Tommy's Monastery. I had two signs, 13 was Jack's lucky number (and he died in 2013—freaky!!) and now this flyer. The universe sent me clear messages that it was time to kick this ugly habit. I have not looked back. There has only been goodness and joy that has come from letting this addiction go. I am so clear, so certain. The things that used to tip me over no longer have my attention. Even my family nonsense is easier to let go of because I see the dysfunction so clearly that I know when to engage and when to let go.

The best way to explain an addiction is that it is a personal hell. I didn't have to change my circle of friends because most of them didn't drink or were responsible drinkers. And the ones who overdid it, I really didn't miss being around. They brought their own set of drama, usually driven by their drinking and now I no longer engage, which brought much more joy into my life. I worked really hard to NOT drink that it was always there looming. When I stopped, those thoughts no longer took up my thoughts. I was free. And I could bring an unencumbered Betsy to the world. No one may have noticed the weight on my shoulders, but it was very present for me and now it's gone, and I love how I feel.

I didn't always love how I felt. My drinking started at age 16 when I was cleaning my brother's apartment. He had a bar in his living room, which was the cool thing to have in a 1970s bachelor pad. I was dusting the top and went behind the back taking notice of each bottle. I pulled out the brand of scotch that my grandfather drank. I opened the bottle and took a whiff of the stink that still today will make my stomach turn. I pulled out a shot glass and poured it to the top like I watched the men in my family do over the years. Quickly, I downed it and almost puked as it stung all the way down. My eyes opened wide and I stood there in shock for a few seconds. Soon after, I felt a warm buzz, which felt kind of nice. Down went another shot and another and another and anything beyond that I don't remember much other than my best friend coming over to rescue me and both my brothers sobering me up before they took me home. Funny thing is, I still remember my first hangover the next day at school. I felt sick all day. That was the start of my journey with alcohol. Again, pretty typical for a teenager to experience alcohol. My college years were five years of partying with little studying. My twenties were another big ol' party that extended into my thirties. I was always able to manage it. Yes, there were the hangovers, the shame of what I did the night before, the getting up and saying to myself, "I'll never do that again," or "I wish I didn't do that." It became my internal hell.

My drinking really took flight the more I allowed my family to make my life hell for following my heart and living my life as a gay woman. I was emotionally battered along with two instances when a family member physically hit me. Apologies came years later along with my forgiveness, but the scars remained. I lived a double life at work, at home, and back and forth in my head. When I was out with my friends, I could be myself and the pain of being "less than" in my family's eyes was washed away with booze. Once I graduated from college and started a professional career, I was driven by wanting to be the best, not only for myself, but there was added effort to excel for family approval. If I was a top producer, a high-income earner, and had all the toys, I could overcompensate for the parts of me that were not approved of in New Jersey. Most times, my heart would break from having my soul be crushed by the lack of acceptance, yet I would put on my happy face and press on like a good daughter, a good sister, and a good employee.

A good buzz would make all the pain go away and the combined socializing in the gay bar made life perfect. I could douse the pain and be where I was fully accepted and receiving accolades that I was more than good enough. Over the years, clubbing felt more depressing than fun; when I had enough, the universe delivered my wonderful wife, Susan, in 1998. Being an artist, she opened up a new world to me that expanded my creative side and thirst for new experiences. The loneliness melted away and there was something about her presence that gave me the confidence to push back at my family. More times than I can count, was I grateful that I moved away from the conditionality that existed from people who I naively thought were my protectors. I found more acceptance from my friends and business colleagues. I wonder, though, if I would have stood up to my family earlier in a firm manner without living a lie, if the quality of my life would have been better, at that time, and if they would have respected me more for standing up for myself. I can't turn back the hands of time, but I am grateful that, after I did stand up for myself and followed my soul, the chains of inner captivity dissolved.

The DUI I received in 1997 was an eye opener that taught me a hard lesson about drinking and driving. I was really lucky. Again, always striving to be the best, I completed the required DUI classes earlier than most, followed whatever was handed to me, and was even asked by the judge to stand in the courtroom and speak about my transformation. He thought I was the attorney given how corporate I was and how I spoke to him in court. I was in a District of Columbia courtroom where I stood out from the other folks there for the same charge. Alcohol does not discriminate by things like gender identity, skin color, social status, or sexual preference. So maybe in the long run, I was handed a gift. At least I was going to find the good because I wasn't going to let this life experience shame me any more than what I allowed my family to do.

As I got older, my drinking was restricted to home or where I knew I didn't have to worry about driving. I always had myself under control at a business function because there was no way I was going to let anyone know I was struggling with addiction. Remember, I felt I already had a black mark against me for being gay. And for most of my career, I did not identify my company as LGBTQ-owned. No way!! So, some evenings, I would come home and have one glass of wine to take the edge off. And there were times where I would go weeks without having any desire to drink. Yet, it was when something got under my skin that coming home to a glass of wine, which often turned into a bottle, took the worry away. After my brothers died, those dark nights were accompanied by sad music sitting in front of the fireplace, which led to a deeper sadness. There were certainly soulful sobs pushed out from the alcohol. Pen and paper were always at hand producing some powerful prose that was an outpouring of my feelings. My wife knew my struggle and she loved me through every step, as well as sitting me down a few times for heart-to-heart talks to register her concern for my drinking. She held the light of faith for me when my light had gone out.

When I finally stopped drinking, a world of clarity opened up. Though I was in my early fifties, it became clearer the nonsense I tolerated over the years by anyone who took issue with me being LGBTQ. It was mostly family related with a few idiots in business, yet it was in my sobriety that I quickly put those people in their place, including family members. Through my inner work, it became more evident that the addiction only stuffed my feelings and held me back from being my true self. Those days quickly came to an end in sobriety and that is why I hope from the depths of my soul that eventually you will give yourself the greatest gift of peeling away all the layers of hurt covered up by your addiction of choice. I promise that your life will be wonderfully better.

It takes a lot of courage to reveal an addiction and it takes even more courage to take back your power over it. I'm proud of the steps I took and take every day to wave at my addiction from a distance. It takes work to overcome addiction of any kind and the first step is the hardest. Simply stopping the addiction scratches the surface. The inner work to drill down the reasons that led me to that point were where my most critical discoveries were nestled. Life started to make sense—the wacky behaviors in my family of origin that ultimately had me flee my home state to find happiness. I thrived from discovering the warts, understood my own actions, and am no longer afraid of the truth. When I get to the truth faster, I can solve the strife that is on my plate, whether in my personal life or business. I am lighter and have more space in my life for more meaningful experiences and I know I am a much more effective leader. Navigating the pressures of business carrying a hangover slowed me down. It wasn't often but often enough to know that I was tired of it. I was a party girl in college and could hang with the best of them throughout most of my life. So, to give it up in my early fifties? I've chalked it up to drinking enough for a lifetime and being ready to create a different future. And it has been a glorious time of life.

Like I said, it takes work to overcome an addiction. Yet, as with anything I have ever set my sights on, the goal was worth the toil. Addiction is an everyday process. For some it's a battle, for some it's a chore, and for some it's a gift. When I look back at old vision boards or a Wish List I had written about ten years ago, ever present was the desire to be sober. So, I am here and I am grateful. And I pray every day to remain sober because it's a priceless gift.

The term "pick your poison" is often used to choose a libation. We have been conditioned that the alcoholic libations put smiles on our face, make us happy, have our tribes bond. The concept does seem fun and serves a purpose until it no longer serves well. If you are striving to excel in some aspect of your life, there is no possible way that overindulgence in any unhealthy form will put you on a path of success or fulfillment. Some learn this early and some take a little longer than others.

We have so many poisons to choose from in our overstimulating world. No longer is just imbibing in too much alcohol that causes problems. Layer on top of that food, caffeine, smartphones, sex, personal development … and the list expands as your environment changes. And notice I have on the list personal development, which one would think is a positive thing. When we hide out behind personal development trainings, organized practices, and people while living the lie of what we perceive is a physically healthy life, are we still covering up the core of what we really need to face?

The labels of what makes an addict go on and on. If these labels put you in a category of some type of alcoholic, you may want to explore deeper. Some of us can shake them off easier than others. Perhaps we are all addicts because we are breathing. I don't know. The fact that I sit here on a Sunday, a day of rest, typing away on my laptop, am I an addict? Ooops, I reached for my cell phone when it made a noise; there goes my addictive behavior again. And I gave up alcohol but have a chai latte almost every day. Walking past the candy dish and not grabbing for a Reese's Peanut Butter Cup makes me feel proud that I took my power back from that bad ol' candy!! Oh, that awesome candy!! One of the benefits of doing inner work is that you can recognize the signs of addiction and have an opportunity to steer away from the people and experiences that cause you strife.

The world of labels and acronyms is, in and of itself, an addiction. Who sits around and comes up with all this stuff anyway? At my stage in life and 30+ years in business and still proudly in the game, I know what doesn't serve me anymore and I can tell you that when I was around people who were toxic frauds was when I drank the most. I needed to tune out their noise or needed to numb out what I knew I needed to do and wasn't ready to shift. When I cleaned out the poisonous people, the other stuff just kind of stopped. There was no need to tune out or avoid. Now, when a toxic person comes into my space, they have no more power. I graciously shift away or the universe seems to blanket me with white light and I'm guided away from their negative energy.

But I just have to say, when I witness toxic behaviors or see someone clearly who is deep in an addiction and I ask how they are and hear a response "I am GREAT," I want to say, "Wake up, people!" You really are not hiding out. The addiction is plain as can be. Some of us hide it better than others, yet, in the shadows the demon is lurking to welcome us into our personal prison. The hardest thing we can do is admit that we are addicts. I challenge you to look in the mirror, stand there for a while, look at yourself and simply ask, "What practice is causing me the most angst OR if I didn't do THIS, what would my life look like?" You know what to insert and it's different for everyone. My name is Betsy and I am an alcoholic. Name the behavior and you owe it to yourself to change it.

In the business world, we are surrounded by social events, networking, booze, drugs, and other stuff thrown in the mix. We have choices and there were times in my earlier years where I didn't always make the right choices. I thought alcohol had my introverted self fit into an extroverted profession. In the end, it came down to self-confidence and it became a lot of work to make sure I didn't drink at certain events. The white knuckling was exhausting and I wanted to be free. I had my last drink in 2015 and since then, it's been the best time of my life. I swear to you. There is no more need to fill a glass and often at functions I have two free hands to have an animated conversation. No more crutch, no more mask … just me and now I like who I see.

So, we all have our poison. It's up to the individual to decide what poison no longer works and sometimes we must do it on our own time. When you are standing back judging, take a good hard look in the mirror and get honest with yourself. What are my poisons and what no longer serves my path? Put a small one aside for a week and see how your life feels. That minor change can bring you much joy and one thing we all can agree on is that we want more joy in life. Go ahead, unpick your poison.

SHAKE IT OFF: *If there is a presence of either a behavior or person that no longer feels good, change it. Write down one addiction you would like to give up and take the steps for one week to change your relationship with it. Don't be afraid of a 12-Step Group. There are plenty out there and you need to test different groups to find the one where your soul feels good. Just take the first step. There will be plenty of support for you. And you have a lot of courage. Let this be the greatest gift you give to yourself because you are worth it.*

Grieving on The Job

Grief I've learned is just love. It's all about love you want to give but cannot. All of the unspent love gathers up in the corners of your eyes, the lump in your throat, and in that hollow part of your chest. Grief is just love with no place to go.

—Anonymous

Grief is a part of life that can't be avoided unless we try desperately to sweep it under the rug. No matter how much we want to not think about it, we can't escape grief. Losing two brothers in 18 months so suddenly was enough to pull the rug out from under me. A few days after burying my brother Tom in 2011, my wife and I were out at a cafe. She could see that I was still in shock, but I wanted to get back into the world outside of funeral homes. We had a wake and funeral services in New Jersey, where most of my family resides and where so many people from Tommy's life lived. Then everyone drove back down to Baltimore so his and my Maryland extended families could pay respects. It was nonstop services for about a week. Right in the middle of services, my company had an important proposal deadline with me as the proposal writer. The government wouldn't give us an extension, so I had to pull a well thought response from my depths and work with my staff at a distance to put the final product together. When I typically am in the trenches with edits and packaging, this time I had to let go and rely on my team to deliver, which they did, and we were awarded the contract.

I was dazed and beyond exhausted and walking through my days on automatic. I can still feel as though my body was an exposed nerve ending operating outside my body. It was as though I were observing the activity inside the cafe and felt as if everyone was looking at me. I had never been paranoid about anything, but those feelings are still embedded in my memory. I kept my eyes down and felt resentment that there was so much joy around me when my heart was broken and my life turned upside down by Tommy's death.

My move to Baltimore in 1987 was much easier with Tommy living ten minutes away. Only twice during the 24 years until his death was he stationed outside of Maryland. We were considered "Cerulo South" and created our own family system that was warm and safe. Every birthday and holiday were spent together whether at our home or at the Monastery. Tommy and I were clear of drama that sometimes reared its ugly head in New Jersey. That made our connection all the stronger because we both hated the conflict. When there was a family event in New Jersey, we typically drove up together while they rarely came down to visit us. I resented that more and more as I got older and to reduce the resentment, I reduced the travel. That was a healthier choice.

Most of us know the feeling when we have to show up to work after bereavement leave. The moment the alarm blasted that morning and it sounded like a blast. My mind quickly asked myself yet again, "Was this past week a nightmare? Am I really putting my feet on the floor to face the world when my whole being is shattered?" Yup, it's time to face the world and being a business owner coming out of the recession, my presence was needed. I had to get back in the saddle, mostly for my employees because, at those moments, I didn't give a crap about myself.

The shower water hit my face that cold January morning with each movement to get dressed feeling like I was in slow motion. I couldn't move any faster. A dark suit was laid out the night before because I was not ready to wear anything with color that could lead anyone to believe that I was okay. C'mon, I am Italian (another label) and we can grieve forever!!! And we are emotional about it. Some of my more dramatic relatives have rushed the coffin and practically jumped in. Really, no kidding!! There is always material for a hearty sitcom in my family!!! I didn't want drama, I just wanted to be sad and not told that "you'll get over it." No, I won't … EVER!! And if I ever do, it will be in my own time.

Into the office I went and gently opened the front door. Tommy had helped us downsize the offices a year before, so his presence was part of the space. My employees have always been the most compassionate group of people because I hire for that quality. I was immediately greeted with warm hugs and love. They were ready to hold me up and told me to take as much time as I needed because we carry each other through the worst of times. I said that staying home would only have me continue crying and I needed healthy distraction. I started my day and my journey to heal.

We can feel our grief and tackle work tasks at the same time. Grief is a part of life and, while our loved ones are gone, we have life to live. If my company was farther along in our recession recovery, I would have taken off more time. The reality was we were in trouble. We had finished up a large contract in 2010 with another one waiting to start that had been canceled in the final hour at no fault of ours. We were a subcontractor. While we had bounced back from the recession, this lost contract put us back in the financial bleeding state. With such a major life-altering event handed to me, financial ruin didn't seem all that bad. I could come back from that, but I could never bring back my brother. In those weeks, I totally got on a much deeper level that life is far more precious than anything business related and that if I could bury my brother then I would overcome the business challenges. Death is very sobering.

I had to balance my grief, my life, and my company's needs as best as I could because there was no luxury in taking a few months off until I felt ready to face the human race. Grief does not have a beginning and end; it is a journey that we must take very seriously and embrace. I made sure I saw my therapist on a regular basis and I attended church many mornings before I went to work. For as much as I find the Catholic faith filled with hypocrisy, the church walls provided much peace. It kept me close to Tommy hearing his favorite songs and readings. I prayed so hard to survive my sadness and the smell of the incense and familiar prayers gave me strength to put one foot in front of the other.

That Sunday, after all the funeral services were complete, I attended mass. On the back of the church bulletin was an advertisement for a grief support group. I swear I had never seen it before because I read those bulletins from front to back. But there it was and, as soon as I got home from church, I called the number. In that same church service, one of the songs was "Be Not Afraid," which was Tommy's favorite hymn that one of his good friends shared during the funeral service. Tommy had sent me a sign on how to get through this and I was listening. How my heart ached to hear his voice again. His cell phone had not yet been turned off, so I called often to hear Tommy's voice.

Grief feels like being hit by a truck and then having it back up over you and then do it all over again every day until it's ready to temporarily park itself. There is no "good time" to grieve and, as business owners and executives, we have to sometimes compartmentalize it and put on the game face to close business deals. I still can't believe I was writing a proposal during the week of Tommy's funeral services. But I did what I had to do. Beulah certainly wasn't going to figure it out and I had lost all trust in that employee. In the end, we won that one-year contract, which was a critical piece of getting us back on a profitable track. I really felt that Tommy was watching over me with that win because it was significant.

Fast forward to June of 2013, when my nephew called to tell me my brother Jack suddenly died of a heart attack. This was surreal. My wife, son, and I had just driven 24 hours from South Florida after cleaning out a condo that I sold as my last connection from Beulah. I still hear the words so clearly from my nephew over the phone. Holy shit, this had to be a bad dream!! I had just been on the phone talking to my best friend about our usual banter and I couldn't believe it when I called her back to tell her. And I started with, "You are not going to fucking believe what I have to tell you!!" She stood with me during Tommy's funeral and she was right there again for Jack. You really discover your true friends during death. And wow, so many people came out to hold me up.

At that point, I truly went into automatic. On little sleep, I packed another bag and we drove to New Jersey. As I walked up to my mother's house, it was like instant replay of it being nighttime, every light beaming from the house with activity. I opened the door to shocked faces and there was my mom in her chair, strong and solid. Hard to explain, but at 89, she was clearly the wise matriarch making sure Jack's family was held up. My mother can go from being the strongest woman I know to pressing those buttons that can break my heart. But there she was, just freaking SOLID. Very grounded, very clear, and certain of how our family would proceed. After I hugged her tightly, I sat with her and she asked me to come close and she whispered, "We will be strong for Cindy and the boys, this is another devastating blow to our family. We will cry together after everyone has paid their condolences." Crap, there were those words again. Almost mirrored exactly how she delivered them when my father died in 1968. The message of "show no emotion" ever present to protect herself. This time around, I was so over it by having to face another loss that I was more pissed at God than saddened by the loss. Why was our family slowly being dismantled? What was the message here? There were so many things going through my head, like:

Why does "blah blah" get to still walk the planet doing shitty
things when both my brothers are gone?
Am I next?
He had a great life, why now?
This is not fair.
God, why did you do this?

And on and on I went. With little sleep and my body in a state
of shock, I walked through another set of services. We were back
to the same funeral home and this was just too weird for me. Jack
was a highly respected and loved person in the community. He
walked in my father's footsteps as a banker and paid attention to
everyone in the community. No request went unanswered and he
always had time for someone in need. Jack took care of everyone he loved from his family, childhood friends, long-time bank
customers, and anyone along the way in need. He carried a lot of
people, helped a lot of people, and, in the end, that all weighed
heavy on him. Just like Tommy, Jack's heart was worn out. He
was my protector, my big brother, and my business confidante.
During the recession when I questioned my own leadership ability
to get us through the tough times, he consistently said, "You will
be stronger on the other side when others are closing up shop. You
know what to do and stick with it." His visit to Baltimore the week
before he died was to congratulate me for sticking with it. In 2009,
we had downsized to a postage stamp office space and, in 2013,
I relocated the office to a new area in a much larger space. Jack
was genuinely happy for my success because he knew I worked
hard to turn it around.

Okay, here I am again, so it was starting to feel like a cake-
walk. And how crazy that multiple deaths should start feeling commonplace for me. I pulled out my trusty *Healing After
Loss: Daily Meditations for Working Through Grief* by Martha
Whitmore Hickman and began my familiar grieving process.

My wife handed me that book after Tommy's death and it became my lifeline during the first year of grieving. Here I was again, turning the pages like a trusted old friend, taking in the words, feeling my pain, and not just grieving Jack, but throwing Tommy back in the mix, too. I journaled like a madwoman every day. I wrote a letter to Tommy and Jack almost every day for a few months. It was my way to feel connected and talk to them about whatever was bothering me. I wrote how much I missed them; wrote about family drama, which always proved entertaining until it didn't; and asked them to pray for me, so I could survive. And there were days I wanted to be with them. I think some of my worst moments with alcohol ended with me crying that I wanted them to come rescue me because the madness was too much to bear. After I became sober, I was so clear and certain that there was a whole hell of a lot of life to be lived and I was staying on earth to live out more dreams.

This time felt more urgent for me. Another sibling gone and we are down to three. Freaked me out. As I was in one of my soulful cries, I felt so deeply in my heart that I had so much more to give on earth, so much more to do, to discover about myself. But what do I do with all these feelings? Getting into "do mode" was not going to be what I needed. I learned so much about myself and life as I grieved. It took losing two cherished people for me to give myself permission to stop, to stay in bed, to eat what I wanted. I can at least say that during that time I packed on weight because my inner response was, "I just lost a brother so I'm going to eat that second piece of cake." On a healthy note, I played on a women's tennis league and became the "comeback kid" because, if there was a shot to get to all I would tell myself was, "If I could get through losing my brother, I can win this point." And I had the best record in the 2011 season. There were many things that would typically have gotten under my skin and I started to pick and choose what was most important to get upset over.

Pissant clients didn't have a chance. And I didn't reach through the phone and castrate them, I kindly said, "That doesn't work for AdNet and I understand if you want to use another firm, but I can't agree to your terms." There was no raised voice or strife. The client ended up seeing it my way and the working relationship transformed into a collaborative partnership. Also, during 2011, I told Beulah it was time to end the business relationship. The last day of her employment became the first day of my freedom. I wasn't scared, there was no second guessing. High-maintenance people contributed to putting both my brothers in an early grave and I used these losses as a learning opportunity. If you caused stress in my life, it was time to clear the clutter. And clear it out, I did.

My health also improved. After Jack died, I registered to run the 2014 New Jersey Half Marathon, not once but the following year as well. It was time to be more conscious of my diet and it really took small changes to see the greatest impact. I saved treats for the weekend and cut back on carbs. I could also feel my grief lifting. The greatest change was giving up alcohol. There were plenty of nights that a bottle of wine and music got me through my sadness. I started to see that I was falling into a depression and leaving my life behind. I hid my addiction well to most people on the outside, but my wife would lose me on those deep nights of sadness. As I blossomed through my recovery, it was quite evident that my alcohol addiction was not about my brother's loss but more so the marginalization from my family over the years.

Recently, we had to let go of all three of our beloved pets in a year timeframe with the most recent being my baby girl, Bleu. It was a devastating time equivalent to when my brothers passed away. The sobbing went on for a few days, I didn't eat and could barely get through the day. Work was a welcomed distraction. I put in place the same things I did when my brothers died, minus alcohol, and faced it head on day by day. This pushed me to update the Bereavement Policy in our Internal Employee Handbook to give time for the loss of a pet. Pets are our family and for those who roll their eyes at us or say, "It's just a dog," all I have to say is, "GET LOST." Be tender with yourself and honor your process. Something majestic will emerge if you give your grief the space to evolve.

If you are willing to take up running, it is such a great release. I inevitably cried through the first mile of every run. And it was cathartic. It was almost as though I was crying out the tears that I hid for decades. My brothers gave me a gift to release the weight I was carrying and, in their deaths, my courage to no longer tolerate anyone who tried to control or bully me. These brothers accepted me, embraced and protected me, so even in their deaths, they still watched over me. It's just not possible to take a swipe at me again or try to dumb me down. Please don't let this sound like we can't have differences of opinion, it's all in the delivery. I have no issue walking away from anyone who is emotionally harmful. It's just not allowed, real simple.

People grieve differently, and I chose resources and tools that could get me back up on my feet quickly because I had a business to run. Most of us don't have the luxury to take a break from the world for a few months to get our wind back. I had to carefully walk through my new life and be especially conscious of whom I had in my space. Now, if I see someone with drama written all over them, my time with that person is limited.

In the workplace, I knew when I had hit a wall of grief. I would simply let my team know. I didn't walk in and make a dramatic declaration, I would just go about my day and if I was in a meeting and not feeling myself, I would just say that I was having a tough day. No drama, just honest sharing. My workplace supports employees through loss and tough life issues. We carry each other through and, for that, we are fortunate to have created a workplace conscious of life events. There is a time and place for emotions, so make no mistake, we have clients to serve but every so often life bites you in the butt and, if for a few moments my team or I become vulnerable and need support, we are there to get each other through.

One of my primary roles is business development. Who the hell wants to sell anything when grief is sitting on your shoulders? If you can delay it, great, but more than likely we have to get back in the saddle. In the first month of my return, I set up sales appointments with clients or people who I knew would be understanding. Most times the issue never came up and I certainly didn't bring it up, but if a client whom I had for years asked the simple question, "How are you?" I shared my loss. I didn't take a lot of time but acknowledged it and conveyed that it's a day-to-day process. Then I got right back to our business conversation. Lots of people avoid grief or just don't know what to say, so they say nothing. It meant the world to me when I received a call, card, email, or a kind smile of understanding through the early weeks. Allow yourself to acknowledge it and if you really want to fall apart, come in late or leave early if you can give yourself the adjustment time.

Here are my suggested practices to support you with loss while enduring workplace demands:

■ If you need to take time beyond corporate bereavement time, ask for it. A good leader will support your healing.

■ Participate in a grief support group. They are offered at hospitals, churches, and community centers. Grief does NOT discriminate, and I got to hear stories from others from all walks of life. We bonded and respected each other through our feelings. Try not to judge yourself or anyone else in a support group. Just show up. That's the secret for most of life's joys. Show up. It turned out this group brought me much hope through both losses.

- Journal your feelings. Give this space to yourself to let the emotions flow.
- Upon returning to your workplace after bereavement leave, be mindful of the meetings you are putting on your schedule. Ask yourself if you are ready to dive into a high-stress meeting. You may be more than fine, but at least ask yourself the question. If the meeting feels over your head, bring a colleague you trust as support or reschedule for the following week. Business owners and senior executives have to jump into the hornets' nest when they break open, so proceed with mindfulness. Grief does not stop for business, so learn how to work with both. You can, just be gentle with yourself.
- If you believe in faith or a higher power, call upon prayer to cradle you through this time. I promise you that prayer and/or meditation works.
- Stay clear of substances that bring you down. A drink might help take the edge off, but it only takes you deeper into despair. Instead of a drink, call a friend. I wasn't always the best with this, but eventually my grief got me sober and that was a gift.
- Don't go too overboard with your diet. Have comfort food while you are healing and be as moderate as you can because, when you surface from the grief, the extra pounds will drag down your energy. Everything in moderation.
- Find books on grief that fit your loss. There is a lot of wisdom and authors can help you validate your feelings to assure you that you are not alone.

SHAKE IT OFF: *Allow your grief to be your permission to slow your pace to honor your loved one. Their memory and your peace are worth the gentle pace in the long run.*

Financial Health

In all realms of life, it takes courage
to stretch your limits, express your power,
and fulfill your potential ... it's no different
in the financial realm.

—Suze Orman

"Save for a rainy day" is what my grandmother always said. Many of our parents and grandparents used this old-fashioned phrase. The simplicity of it is more valuable than a successful stock pick. When I started my company in 1990, at 28, I had guts to give it my best shot and not enough of a nest egg built up to lose if my venture failed. I took my 401(k), savings, and credit cards and AdNet was born. At every turn, I socked money away because debt just makes me crazy. There is no reason for it with good planning and wise choices. Thank God I had the wisdom to acquire about four different credit cards with sizable credit lines in 1990, because that became my working capital in the early years. Banks weren't giving money to women to start businesses back then. The male bankers were lousy creeps who did everything they could to keep us down. Not the credit card companies!! They were in the business to make money and didn't discriminate. It's clearly a much smarter business model to make money rather than relying on discriminating Causasian male bankers who looked down their noses at bright-eyed business women with dreams and solid business plans. That didn't seem to be enough for the creeps. Most of the male bankers who were doling out money to their good ol' boy networks weren't the high-paid bankers and certainly weren't rolling in cash. They just didn't want to see women do better than themselves.

But not this businesswoman. No one was going to get in my way, not then, not now, not ever. Because I had a dream that was far bigger than any wall that was put on my path. My goal was always to bust through any wall that stood in my way and bust I did. The difference between women in business versus men in business, we had to and still have to push harder. Let's focus on how to use financial health to outsmart the jerks who get in our way. The best revenge toward anyone who has tried to hold you back is to go out there to be successful.

It still baffles me when spouses don't know the financial state of their marriage. The role of money has traditionally been the job of the guy in the relationship. Fortunately, women are taking more active roles now that they hold the reins equally, if not more, than their husbands. It has become more of a partnership. For the older generations who still find comfort in the old model, women don't have an equal handle on the finances. I have seen many female friends left with nothing or swindled out of their share because hubby hid the kitty, or the wife had no idea what was in the kitty. My wife and I have our investments together and individually, both names are on accounts, we meet with our financial adviser together, and we regularly review our respective portfolios, so we always know where we are financially. Though we plan to live a long life together, we want to make sure that the other is "in the know" of the finances, should there be a life-threatening event. It's just smart coupleship behavior.

It's unsettling to see people focus on "how it looks" to take on more financial debt. Debt = Stress. Why can't people figure out that simple formula? It's not rocket science. Save more than you spend and you will have more ease in your life. As a small business owner, my approach to saving money has simply saved my personal assets and my company during economic downturns. Since I started AdNet, I had and continue to have the good fortune to build wealth and live with more than enough while keeping expenses reasonable. The 2008 recession threw all my smart savings out the window and I was burning through cash and liquidating investments at every turn. I guess there were choices to close the company and find a corporate job, yet I believed in what AdNet stood for with every fiber of my being that shutting down was not an option. Once the bleeding stopped and the toxicity was exited from the culture, my resolve to rebuild was unstoppable. Finding people employment was one of the most important topics in the economy and I am excellent at what I do, so AdNet had to succeed. It was not an option to give up. Here I was in my late forties, almost starting over.

Thank God for my wife!! The Queen of Coupons, who still can stretch a penny farther than anyone I know. As I went without a substantial salary for two years and my personal savings was at my all-time low, we actually led a wonderful quality of life because we kept our lifestyle simple. The Bank of Betsy was officially closed. No more enabling to anyone who was capable. They had to fend for themselves. Never once was a personal bill or mortgage late. I had a year of salary in my savings account plus our investments and retirement. When money experts tell you to have anywhere from a minimum of three to nine or more months of salary in the bank, listen people, they know what they are talking about. That practice saved me. And it taught me to say "no" to people who could provide for themselves. I wasn't rescuing anyone anymore. If you were an adult, figure it out the same way I figured it out. Turns out that philosophy did more than save me money, it taught me to stop taking care of people. The enabling stopped and I felt liberated. No more was I held hostage by other people's irresponsibility or greed.

While the recession was a defining moment in business for many of us, it taught me priceless lessons that I still hold very close. Today, I still have a chunk of money automatically transferred to a money market account each month. I read Motley Fool and Dent Research to learn ideal stocks to invest. On my own, I have several good picks and a few clunkers here and there. That's why, when I invest, I always ask myself, "Am I prepared to lose this amount of money?" I was always fascinated with Twitter and, as the price per share was falling, I decided to buy it especially after Donald Trump won the election. He used Twitter as an effective marketing resource to get the public's attention. The more negativity I saw coming out of Twitter, the more I had an ethical conflict about how Twitter was being used. So, I sold it at a minimal loss. It started to go back up over the past year and when I calculate what I could have earned from the initial investment, I stop and get back in touch with my ethical standards and then am at peace with my decision to sell it at a loss. Sometimes, investments hold moral value to us that exceed the monetary gain or loss. When we invest with a moral compass, I believe the world will prosper more than if we keep feeding the behemoth companies or abuse the environment and people. When we do good with our money our money will, in turn, do good for us.

I have seen people work so hard to keep up with outward perception as they have lost businesses … all because of ego. If you see a downward shift in your business, that is not the time to go out and make large purchases and think the money will show up. Don't act like an egotistical moron. Make prudent purchases. Save the seasons sports tickets for another time, leave the high-end luxury car on the lot, and please don't upsize your home. As business owners, we all want to feel like we can have some fun with the toil we put in our businesses. And rightfully so, but make mindful purchases. I purchased a used luxury car after months of hunting for a good price. We are the stewards of a spacious

170-year-old farmhouse, which we purchased when the market was affordable. Our mortgage is lower than most people's rent payments and that freedom allowed us to build a second home in the mountains where you can hear yourself think. During that process, we designed a modest-size, unique home with most of the products repurposed that we had been storing away for the past ten years once we started to dream about a home in the mountains. Our next move is to downsize our current house and move toward water. We want to be house happy versus mortgage poor. Again, we have freedom because we purchase mindfully and save our money.

It's also important not to be fearful of spending. I see plenty of people live in scarcity that weighs them down. It's hard to live in a "lack of" conversation. More than likely, those individuals are also lacking elsewhere in life, which could seem to be weighed down by whatever they have created. Notice my use of "*they have created.*" You see, financial health is a choice. People don't have to be millionaires to have wealth. It's about your relationship with money. For some people, living modestly, driving an old car, wearing comfortable clothes, and enjoying simple things IS wealth. Don't kid yourself to think that all millionaires are happy. I have certainly had wealth and been miserable. After I lost my wealth, was when I had a different relationship with money as I built my bank account back up. I saw the pain and stress I was under and, this time around, I wanted a quality life over a quantity bank account. As it turned out, when I freed myself of the chase for more money, it started to accumulate organically.

Don't get me wrong, I stress when business revenue is not where it should be and I lose sleep when there are employee issues, so I don't want you to think that I sit in a meditative state counting my gold. Somehow, I wish that was the case, but the reality is. that as a small business owner, we seem to be "on call" or "at attention" 24/7. And I'm used to it after 30 years. This time is different because at 59, I make different choices and I know that living in stress is not healthy. Remember, two of my brothers died of heart attacks at 59 and 62, so it's imperative that I changed my relationship with people and behaviors that caused over-the-top stress.

Part of what keeps me grounded is keeping healthy personal finances at all times. That balances out periodic roller coaster trends in business. If you want more peace in your life, take out a piece of paper and have a truth session with your personal spending habits. Are you addicted to spending money? Do you spend too much money on alcohol/food/clothes/toys? When you want to lose weight, a nutritionist will tell you to write down everything you eat to get a clear picture of your eating habits. So, I'm telling you to write down every time you spend money. If you don't have time to write it down, take out your cell phone and snap a picture of the receipt or where you spent the money. Create an album under your pictures and save the photos in the album to help you keep track of spending or download a receipts app. You may discover some interesting spending habits. If Amazon is becoming your best friend, look at what you are buying.

Ask yourself these questions:

- How badly do I need this item?
- Does my health depend on this purchase?
- Did I get the best price for the purchase?
- Can I live without this item?
- How many of this item do I already have?
- What mood was I in when I made the purchase?

Just pay attention to the answers. You might be surprised by them. There was a time that I ordered books left and right, yet the pile of unread books became much higher than the finished reading pile. So, I got smart and went to the library. That saved me money on buying books and gave me a set amount of time to read the book, which allowed me to be more focused. I only took out what I really wanted to read. Boy, did I save load of money on book/DVD/CD purchases. It was a small change, but my pennies started to turn into dollars in the bank. My monthly game is how low can I get my credit card balance. I pay off my credit cards monthly, so when I have a credit card bill that is super close to $0, that makes me smile. I not only saved money, but I saved on clutter space. I recently saw a friend over Facebook use a term "Go Big or Go Home" when sharing about a purchase. You keep going and there may be NO home to go to!!

Let's take a look at your business. Have you taken time to go through your Vendor List to see what you are spending money on? Our biggest culprit was business insurance. Our vendor took us for granted having been a customer for 15 years. They never shopped our coverage. So, I shopped brokers and found better prices. Turned out, the vendor was a Slick Willy and I kicked him out the door in one year. I chose an LGBTQ woman for our next vendor and she shops coverage and gives us great prices. That, in turn, had me keep going down the list and boot out any vendor who did not give us the same level of service we give to our clients. Where I could, I chose women and diverse vendors. Women have to put our money where our mouths are and give business to other women. And, if you are LGBTQ, then give your business to LGBTQ vendors. If I have an extraordinary vendor who gives me great service and price, gender does not matter. For me to give my clients the best, my vendors are my partners and they have to be the best.

Remember a few chapters back, I shared with you a story about my experience with bankers. Shop them annually to see where you can get the best service. I had been with the same bank for a long time and, though the relationship was good, they would not join the Maryland LGBT Chamber of Commerce. That didn't work for me. Time for a change, so I moved to a fabulous banking partner who fully supports the LGBTQ community. That feels like good business!!

SHAKE IT OFF: *Monitor your expenses for 30 days to see where you can trim the waste. Less Waste = Less Clutter = More Spiritual + Financial Wealth.*

V. YOUR FINISH LINE

Risk = Reward

If you have a dream and it means
that much to you, take it all the way.

—Me

Whatever you determine your finish line to be, whether that is an important project, your career path or a new business venture; anything you take on that is new requires risk. Can't get around it. So, you might as well make it a joyful process because your positive and "can-do" attitude will make even the ugliest of steps more tolerable.

Earlier in my career, one of my male bosses subtly pushed me to overcome my fears as I entered the world of executive recruiting. He would say that if you don't take a risk, you won't feel the reward. And Sam was right. The only way to get to the gold in whatever life experience you are striving to reach is to go outside what feels comfortable. We have all heard terms such as, *comfort zone*, *outside the box*, or *on the skinny branches*, to name a few. Every person has a different comfort zone in their fiber and we have to know ourselves to understand the point that we push through to reach a sense of accomplishment. I adapted Risk = Reward as a positive mantra to guide me through my career and it has never failed me in any effort or dream.

I will get a quiver in my stomach that turns into a big knot depending on my level of discomfort. The feeling will move up and settle in my chest if it's a major stressor, which then triggers for me that I have to do something differently more urgently. The butterflies flapping around my stomach are easier to manage. Wherever that feeling lands, I'm going to take an action to restore my sense of balance. When I have the physical sensations in my gut, I'm in the middle of a new risk. For instance, I was presented an opportunity to acquire several pieces of new business over the past year that had components that were outside my business comfort zone. In order to fulfill my organization's forecast and future vision, I have to approach growth differently. These particular opportunities were new for the business and me. It would have been easier for me to stay the same and do what I know. But to accelerate my vision, the need for risk was necessary.

When I am in the middle of risk, I list the positives and the worst-case scenarios—just freakin' do it!!! Once I have my list, I talk it through in depth and often at nauseum with trusted colleagues. This is where belonging to a group for business owners allows you the confidential space to give voice to your plan and hear honest feedback. Be prepared for input you didn't expect that could send you back to the drawing board or abandon the plan all together. At this point, listen with an open mind and take your next move.

If you find yourself passing by opportunities because the risks are too much for you, it may be time to re-evaluate where you want to go. Look, rewards can come with little to no risk, yet if you want to be bold to move to a new level, you have to feel uncomfortable. Lost sleep has been a regular occurrence for me this year because I have wrestled with strategies in the middle of the night. Or I go to bed with my mind racing. These are the by-products of leadership. Yet, on the other side of these opportunities are valuable rewards. Feeling uncomfortable to the point when I would like to throw up is a part of the journey. If you want that reward, you have to take the risk. There's no avoiding it.

Many of my business decisions will start with formulating a strategy. I follow my tried and true practice of taking out a pad or my journal, grab my pen, and start writing. Use whatever modality you like. At the top of the page I clearly write out the issue or goal that I need to move to a new level, then at the bottom of the page I write out my desired outcome. The road map to my goal is designed through the words I write in between the issue and the outcome. The plan contains strategy and risk. And the words are unfiltered to allow me to identify the experiences I may encounter along the way. There is no way I can take my goal to a new level if I keep doing the same thing. My wife uses a great phrase from Al Anon: "You keep doing what you are doing, you will keep getting what you are getting!!" There is no way you can take your business or your life to a new level if you keep doing the "same ol' same ol' " every day. You have to take risks!! Well, you really don't have to take any risks and if you are totally okay with where your life is at, then you are good to go. I am sure there will be a time in my life when I have taken enough risks and will be very content enjoying the rewards from years of risks.

My process works for a business plan, a well-being plan, a retirement plan, a divorce, etc. I wrote out my dream for the perfect spouse (we have been together since 1998 and married since 2013), our home, and the path to rebranding my company. All of those "dreams" are my reality. *If you want it, dream it, write it, and go get it!!*

For now, here is a sample of my worksheet. I promise by the end of the process, my road map is created and inevitably my risks get me to the reward.

▪ ▪ ▪

RISK = REWARD PLAN

CHALLENGE: Write out the challenge in detail. This is your plan, so no need to abbreviate or be brief. Be clear and honest.

Timeline: When will the outcome be reached?

I. What am I afraid of?

_____

_____

_____

_____

_____

II. What would _____ look like if I overcame this challenge?

_____

_____

_____

_____

_____

III. What do I need to overcome in myself to reach my outcome?

_____

_____

_____

_____

_____

IV. Who do I need to involve/engage to accomplish my plan?

_____

_____

_____

_____

_____

V. What are the steps that I need to take to accomplish my plan?

_____   By when:

_____   By when:

_____   By when:

_____   By when:

_____   By when:

_____   By when:

_____   By when:

_____   By when:

_____   By when:

_____   By when:

VI. Check-in: How am I doing? (Based on your end date, build in several check-ins to see how you are doing. Sometimes this plan is urgent where I need to take immediate action and other instances where the outcome is accomplished in a one-, three-, or six-month timeline.)

What action steps need to be changed?

Do my "By When" dates need to be adjusted?

OUTCOME: Write down the EXACT desired result. Be clear and honest.

■　　■　　■

Congratulations!! You wrote out your plan. As women in business, we have to be fast and flexible to get things done. There are times we fly by the seat of our pants. When I have taken quality quiet time to plan, I get to where I need to go. Being in business since 1990 takes a lot of resilience and planning to make it all work through economic and life changes.

An effective business owner and leader requires many components to make solid decisions. Accurate reporting is a key factor because knowing your numbers is critical. I'm not going to use the term "numbers don't lie" because we have certainly seen business scandals created as a result of lying about the numbers. When you have accurate reporting, you can quickly see your company's strengths and weaknesses. There are many times I feel the numbers of my company before I see the financial statements. No, I don't have any magic powers; I keenly observe daily wins and challenges across my team and we discuss goals every week. So, the gross numbers are no secret and since I negotiated most of the vendor contracts, I know our ballpark monthly costs. A good small business owner needs to have a pulse on the financial health of their organization. That has allowed me to squirrel money away for the rainy days and anticipate the dips, so the organization is not overstressed.

To succeed long term in business, I have taken risks and taken steps to avoid risky transactions. It's a delicate dance to know when to say move forward, when to pause, and when to terminate a business relationship. Through some of my most gut-wrenching challenges, I have learned that getting myself in and out of a hornet's nest has produced some of my best growth strategies. None of these events were done by only me. Depending on the nature of what needs to get accomplished, my team is right there with me. In 30 years, I have had many people work for my company with way more outstanding and gifted individuals than bad apples. During those times, I would sometime present the challenge and we build the plan together. I also have created the plan myself and come into a meeting to create another plan and then look at the input from my staff. There are certain challenges where they are closer to the issue than I am and vice versa.

That is why not only pushing yourself as the leader to take new risks is important but more important is guiding your team to take risks. Hey, an owner is not supposed to be good at everything. We hire people who bring talents that we need to move the dream forward. I love the saying "Teamwork Makes the Dream Work," which one of my youngest employees turned me onto. She is so right!!! When I risk, my team sees that, and they take risks. When I see my team take risks, that gets me in risk mode to stretch beyond what I know.

The way I look at it, the more well-thought risks you take, the more rewards are out there for you to receive. There is no way you can grow a business by standing still. I have overcome many challenges and stops and starts only to come out on the other side stronger; maybe a little more tired, but strong and energized (with a good night's sleep after we have accomplished our goal).

SHAKE IT OFF: *Having an effective plan requires taking time to stop, think, write, and act. A plan with no action gets you nowhere. Your actions will determine your rewards. And you are worth it!!*

Legacy

You want to be part of something like that,
that's something bigger than yourself,
that's something you leave a legacy of
being part of something special.

—Saquon Barkley

As I have developed my leadership into my fifties, legacy is more prevalent in my thinking and actions. I reflect on "have I and how can I make the world a better place during my time on our earth?" I have been given this precious gift called life and it is something I value greatly as I have seen people close to me lose their lives way too soon. The choices I have made since 2011 come with more well-thought action. So many people before me allowed for me to have greater opportunities, which is why it's important to pay it forward to the up-and-coming generations. Our world continues to be in a precarious place with a multitude of human rights being questioned. If you are part of a diverse group, the fights that we thought were won are now back under the microscope to be dissected. While this has been upsetting and will give me cause for pensiveness, rather than be complacent, I have put forth more of my energy toward positive change.

In 2012, after I was certified as an LGBT Enterprise through the National Gay and Lesbian Chamber of Commerce, I attended my first NGLCC Annual Leadership Conference in the summer of 2013. I had just lost my second brother the month before and was still raw, yet I felt really safe being at a conference where I could bring forth my total self. My wife and I were in the process of planning our September wedding and I was in the company of business people who were sharing some of their own wedding plans. I felt so proud to share my joy with other people with no worry of weird looks. It was absolute freedom.

Attending the various luncheon programs, announcements, and awards were given for the various LGBT Chambers of Commerce across the United States. At the time, approximately 35 were in existence. I was riveted by the accomplishments shared and the passion that exuded from the members who created successful Chambers from scratch. "Maryland needs a Chamber," were the words going through my head that week. Fast forward to 2014's and 2015's Annual Conference and again I witnessed new Chambers having been formed with people proudly gathered on stage to accept awards. Only this time, I closed my eyes and pictured myself with a group of Maryland business people on stage being recognized for our work. I held that vision and it resonated deeply in my heart that it was time to take a leap of faith and roll up my sleeves to make a new dream come true.

Conversations started at the end of 2015 with my co-founder and I gathering LGBTQ business owners and executives to test the waters. The group of 30 were all in and the journey began. Several times, I backed away because I knew this was a time-intensive commitment because we were basically starting a new nonprofit entity, a new business to serve Maryland LGBTQ business owners. Somehow, each time I spoke the words that I don't have the bandwidth to take this on, the journey seemed to organically continue. I took on the role of president. After being closeted in my professional career for over 25 years, the universe was calling me forth to be fully authentic everywhere in my life and, while I felt exhilarated, I was scared to death. The list of what-ifs went through my head; what if my clients no longer want to work with AdNet? What if business people were snickering behind my back? What if no one joined? What if I could not juggle the work required as I was running my company? What if the venture failed and what if after bringing people together, I failed as a leader? These thoughts repeated in my head as a continuous loop each time our group met for planning sessions. My wife, always being supportive, asked me, "Are you sure you want to take this on, NOW? Your plate is already full." My answer was clearly, "Yes," because once I start something, I take it to completion often turning myself and her inside out along the way.

June 2017 was the official launch of the Maryland LGBT Chamber of Commerce (www.mdlgbt.org) and the dream was really real, complete with an amazing group of committed people who turned themselves inside out to see us grow. After more than one year in existence, we had attracted over 100 paid members, an impressive list of large corporate sponsors, and continued to put on vibrant programs that helped the business community grow. I am in awe of what this group has created. My term as president ended after one year and I was happy to pass the torch to an incredible new Board of Directors to take the Chamber to the next level of growth. In my new role as an advisor, I focus on exploring which legislative issues will give the LGBTQ business community in Maryland an equal voice to win contracts. All we want is a chance to bring our best selves to our clients. I'll say it until I am blue in the face, "You can open the door of opportunity because I am a diverse supplier but what keeps me in the door long term is because I give my clients the best service." In August of 2018, our Chamber received the NGLCC Rising Star Chamber Award. We were very relevant and people noticed. That confirmed in my heart that my leap of faith in 2016 was worth the work. This Chamber will continue to grow and evolve for years to come because gifted leaders are carrying on its mission.

The recent years of my life have tested my resilience in balancing my company, starting a new Chamber of Commerce, writing this book, and having a life somewhere in the midst of my pace. Sometimes, we get few chances to leave our mark and this is my time to create my legacy to help open doors in business and open minds of ignorance. Your legacy can be how you raise your kids and how you lead them to living a good life. It can be starting/growing a business as well as being an empowering manager at your company. The list is numerous. It's how you show up in the world that can determine your legacy. It really does not have to be a dramatic event, but it should have meaning in your heart. You are leaving some type of imprint on the world after you step away from the experience that inspired you to step outside of a comfort zone. An experience is creating the future. That is legacy and it's personal.

Our world is in serious trouble, so imagine if many people took time to leave an organization stronger, put together a group that brings joy to people once a month in a chaotic world. What if someone writes down a roadmap to help others heal from cancer or learn how to support a loved one on that journey? What a difference that would make; it could be life defining. That is legacy. When something you have done has had a light of inspiration go off for another human being or gave them a job where they can provide for their family, that is legacy. Don't let the media make you think that legacy is only for the rich and powerful. True legacy starts at the grassroots with an idea that builds into a result where you have done something that impacts others for the good. It can be in your neighborhood, your circle of friends, your community. It can be simple or elaborate and everything in between.

This is when you take some quiet time and paper and pen and write. It goes like this:

IF YOU COULD PICK ANYTHING THAT MATTERED ENOUGH TO MAKE YOUR LIFE OR THE WORLD A BETTER PLACE, WHAT WOULD IT BE?

_____

_____

_____

_____

_____

WHAT DIFFERENCE WOULD YOU WANT TO MAKE FOR THE UP-AND-COMING GENERATION?

_____

_____

_____

_____

_____

Sometimes you don't know what you really want to do until you put yourself somewhere that may inspire you. If you told me in 2016 that I would be a founder of a successful Chamber of Commerce that opened doors for the LGBTQ business community, I would have told you that there was no way that I could find the time or that I would have a clue of how to get people to join. Legacy does not mean that you do it yourself. Collaboration allows you to dream bigger and see ideas come to fruition sooner. Once you put a thought out there, people start to show up and often have similar ideas and don't know where to start. Once you speak about these inspiring acts of legacy, you will find that you start to attract people who are aligned with your goal. Speaking about your idea allows it to take shape and become more beautiful when more people put their imprint on your idea.

Because of one conversation, Maryland has a robust and growing Chamber of Commerce that is driven to connecting high-quality LGBTQ businesses with corporations and each other. We are working on legislation to expand our business reach in Maryland. This was not a reality four years ago and now the entity is thriving. And that was done at age 55. So, don't ever let your age stop you from your legacy. It's just a number and with age we have much more wisdom to bring to the party.

There will come a day within the next ten years that I will step away from leading my company. And when that day comes, I can leave the helm knowing that I provided a caring workplace (post-Beulah) where I led with compassion and integrity. Being successful can be measured by how much money is in the bank, how many expensive toys you have, and the size of your home when, in truth, that is certainly about ego. And you can be humble, have an ego and be successful at the same time. It comes down to the question: Will you run your ego, or will your ego run you? Ego is part of our self-confidence and self-esteem, which you need a healthy dose of when you run a business. But if ego evolves into self-importance, you can go down a painful slippery slope.

When all that is put aside, as it should be in this egotistical world, my success is defined by being a smart small business owner who provides a caring and emotionally healthy workplace for my employees on and off site. I have accomplished what I set out to do 30+ years ago when I started my company, which was to be more caring in a cutthroat industry. Accomplished. To be successful in a male-oriented line of business within the recruiting industry. Accomplished. Make the kind of living that gave me the things my family and I needed and wanted. Accomplished. Become a published author. Accomplished. Sober. Joyfully Accomplished.

There are plenty more dreams for me to fulfill before I leave the planet. My next dream is to spread the message of empowerment to diverse communities through this book and write my next book, *The Beulah Syndrome*, to teach business owners and leaders to watch for the signs of dysfunction and how to rid their workplace of the dreaded Beulah and we all have them!!

So, what will your legacy be?

SHAKE IT OFF: *If there is a nagging passion in your heart to leave the world a better place, take the time to put yourself in places that will tap into your inspiration, name it, dream it, and make it real.*

The Finish Line

*It's never too late—never too late to start over,
never too late to be happy ...*

—Jane Fonda

I keep moving my finish line farther because, every year, there is a new dream for me to reach. The idea of retirement looming within the next ten years is something that has snuck up on me. My soul still feels like a kid always learning new things and craving new experiences. Having a finish line for this leg of your career is wise to explore.

I have multiple finish lines based on my life's interests and you can, too. You may be at a point in your current career that you are ready to take the leap to another adventure, thus putting completion on your corporate job and starting a business that takes you to your retirement. You may want to transition your business and go work for a company until retirement and you may simply be ready to leave the life of work and pursue a joyful path. Whatever it may be, write your dreams—big or small—on paper and chase them until you live them.

At 52, I put my sights on completing a Half Marathon. At the time, my thinking was, am I even in shape to run a 13.1-mile race? No, I wasn't but I got in shape. To receive a medal, I had to cross the finish line in 3 hours and 15 minutes. I completed the race in 2 hours and 36 minutes. Pretty respectable for a first-time runner in my fifties. I was so empowered by the experience, I ran it again the next year and with far less training, finished the race in 2 hours and 32 minutes. My dream goal is to run the New Jersey Half Marathon again in 2022 and, at age 60, complete the race in less than 2 hours and 30 minutes. Though older, I know I can accomplish that because of my sheer will to reach my goal. For today, doing shorter races and enjoying the experience will keep me satisfied until 2022.

Success for me in business is no longer about money. That clouds my journey and I am very clear on where I am headed. To have a workplace that is healthy with a diverse team of people with integrity who are driven by each other's success along with their own is very important on my goal list. When I FINALLY got in touch with the fact that I am a really good small business owner who puts compassion alongside of results, I achieved my dreams. There will always be one more contract to win, one more client to please, and one more employee to champion. That's part of having a sustainable and growing business. But at the core of my company has always been my desire to have a strong foundation of people who care deeply about doing the right thing. We may not always get it right the first time, yet we stay with our process to treat people and each other with respect. We make a difference in our community and our work is meaningful.

In 2016, the time seemed right to have a Chamber of Commerce in Maryland focused on building the LGBTQ business community. There were a lot of moving parts required to tackle this type of endeavor but passionate people stepped into the vision to make it real through volunteer people-power. At times, I felt like a rubber band over-stretched yet it forced me to manage my time more efficiently and ask for help to juggle the demands successfully. My mind rarely rested at night as my thoughts would bounce from AdNet to the Chamber, to our life and it took a lot of work to quiet my mind. As I sit here as a past president, I am grateful to have completed a successful term and even more proud to pass the torch to a group of very talented business owners who will put their imprint in place and continue to grow this much-needed entity.

In 2018, I was honored with receiving an award called Leaders in Diversity in the Baltimore business community. Having taken a stand for diverse populations is something that has been part of my fiber for many years, only it is in the past five years that I have devoted much time to advocacy. I'm telling you, something happened for me as I walked into my fifties. There are many people who get the calling for advocacy much younger. But the bug really bit me later in life and, with my life experiences under my belt and freedom from shedding dysfunctional people and practices, I was able to hear the call, got moving and scratching the surface of who I am capable of being. Now I get to continue to blossom and grow my advocacy efforts beyond Maryland because there is much to do to help heal our world. Even if you think you have a small voice or very little time to give, add up all the small voices and the little bits of time to give and we have a magnificent effort toward change.

Early on in this book, I shared how I said to my coach that I was uncomfortable with being comfortable in my career. And every day that I am in automatic on the hamster wheel called business, I remind myself that there is still so much more meant for me ahead. Age is my inspiration, my teacher, and my friend. Now I am having conversations on how to accomplish more dreams in a gentler way that supports the changes in my body and my psyche. I no longer want to reach a goal just for the sake of grabbing another brass ring. I have more than enough in my collection, with some more meaningful than others. When I look back on my career, it is the journey in my fifties that unleashed my soul. I drew upon my courage to speak up for what I needed and speak out for what is fair and equitable.

I adore the younger generations for their outspoken views and basically, they are not settling for the pace and opinion created by the Baby Boomer generation. We get to collaborate and make change and I look forward to continuing my journey of growth and reaching beyond what I thought possible. You see, I have set up many finish lines along the way and I'll never truly be done until the universe says it's time. Until that point, I will give my fullest effort to lead the way the best way I can and use my labels honorably and proudly to open doors for those who are up-and-coming. And for my peers who hear a little voice speaking from their soul to take a risk to try something new, I'll be the reassuring presence to gently nudge you forward. I promise to continue to call out inequities as I see them and speak out for what is truly right. And no matter who or what tries to push me down, I'll shake if off, get back up, and cross the finish line—again and again!!!

SHAKE IT OFF: *The finish line keeps moving with each new venture that comes my way. Never stop taking those steps, even when it's freaking you out. Eventually, your fear will transform to determination and inspiration. And when you cross each finish line—and I hope for you there will be many—your victory will be sweet and your soul will thank you for taking you on the ride of your life.*

Hire Betsy to Train and Speak to Your Team

Having been in leadership roles for many years, I have experienced a wide range of styles from empowering to narcissist bullies. My approach in leading these conversations includes passion, sincerity, and humor. As I share my journey, I want to hear what inspires you and what you are afraid of that may keep you from reaching your dreams and goals. I make it a safe place for sharing by laughing at my own mistakes, so you will share yours, too!!

Presentations are in-person and virtually for however many people you want to bring together.

Let us explore together how I can serve your teams best—whether that is through a customized training, individual leadership coaching, or public speaking. Reach out to me in the following ways:

Phone: 443-629-9046
Email: info@betsycerulo.com
Website: www.betsycerulo.com
LinkedIn: https://www.linkedin.com/in/betsycerulo/

Acknowledgments

Thank you to Jenn Grace, CEO of Publish Your Purpose Press, for "seeing" my story and helping me to breathe life into this book. I can't tell you how many times I would start and stop thinking this book would never be finished. You helped me overcome my fear and my "not enough" stuff. The PYP team of Lisa Corrado, Niki Garcia, Heather Habelka, Karen Ang, and Nan Price were the "Shake It Off" team who patiently checked in, pushed, and nudged me to cross the finish line. Yeah, we did it!!

My son, Matt Gifford, captured the essence of my journey through his artwork. Thank you, Matt, for making the cover come alive. Your art inspires me to never give up exploring my inner artist. Love you.

I'm honored that the beginning of *Shake It Off Leadership* begins with Lisa Carreño's heartfelt foreword. Lisa, who would have thought that our "snap out of it" moment at the bus station in Fredericksburg in 1983 would get me back on track and save my butt. Your brave words summed up how our coming out instilled the courage in our souls to declare who we are and support others to do the same. I continue to marvel at your fearlessness. You helped me set the stage for my career and offered your gentle encouragement to support me as I got AdNet off the ground. And 38 years later, after we both walked through the bliss and fear of coming out, our friendship stands strong through whatever life sends our way.

I humbly thank all the employees of AdNet over our 30+ years together who challenged, taught, called me forth, and loved me through our victories and losses. Our work is a collective success and could only have happened because of the bonds of trust we built together. Since we redesigned our culture after 2012, we proved how genuine compassion and love for each other could really happen in a corporate environment and be profitable. Thank you, Laura, for holding that vision for many years.

Thank you to Justin, Sam, Jonathan, Ann, Richard, Betty, Frank, and Mary for giving your precious time to write a testimonial. Who you all are in the world as leaders and human beings inspires me every day to keep going.

To my friends from childhood, high school, and college (Ryan and Spellman Hall) who loved and supported me unconditionally at a time when being gay was a tough choice in the early 1980s. It was our heartfelt talks and hugs when I cried that gave me the courage to honor my path. I can't even begin to tell all of you how, when some of those times seemed hopeless, you carried me through. I love you!!! To all my clients and business connections who have become trusted friends, thanks for having my back as I s-l-o-w-l-y opened up about being LGBTQ. Our work together continues to keep me inspired in this crazy world of work.

Mom, through the best and the worst, you taught me resilience and to never give up. I love you unconditionally, no matter what. Daddy, from heaven, I hear you whisper in my ear all the time that I can do it. Thank you for instilling in me to always do the right thing, even when it was heart-wrenching.

I thank God who protected me and made me stronger as I opted for the road less traveled along the way. Keeping my eyes on You as I struggled gave me hope that I would always make it through, even when it felt like I was gasping for air.

Saving the best for last … Susan, my wife and best friend, the night you taught me The Serenity Prayer my life transformed and you breathed hope back into my soul when I thought I had nothing left to give. Thank you for being so patient and loving through every ride I ask you to take with me. Our wedding day in 2013, speaking our vows as we looked deeply into each other's eyes, was truly the happiest day of my life and it keeps getting better and better. I love you more than any words I could ever speak or write. Forever and always.

About the Author

Betsy Cerulo is the CEO of AdNet/AccountNet, a successful certified LGBTE, WBE and 8(a) management consulting firm focused on professional staffing and executive search, based in Baltimore, Maryland, and Co-Founder of the Maryland LGBT Chamber of Commerce. Betsy is the author of *Miss Crabapple and Her Magical Violin*, a children's book that was inspired by lighting up a dream for a child through their imagination. She is also a contributing author of two compilations: *Women Living Consciously* and *Keys to Conscious Business Growth*.

Betsy lives in Baltimore with her wife, Susan, and their treasured Weimaraner, Grace Kelly. Their son and daughter-in-law, daughter, and three grandchildren complete the picture with lots of love, creativity, and laughter.

www.ingramcontent.com/pod-product-compliance
Lightning Source LLC
Chambersburg PA
CBHW051212090426
42742CB00021B/3424